Praise for
Fight
by Kenny Luck

"I felt like I was reading a Tom Clancy book on spiritual warfare. An enjoyable read on a deadly serious subject. You won't be disappointed."

—DAVID MURROW, author, *Why Men Hate Going to Church*

"*Fight* is all about a radically alternative way to fight the good fight against the forces of evil in order to finish well with victory! Kenny Luck got my adrenaline pumping. *Fight* is a 'gotta' read for every Christ warrior."

—DR. WALT KALLESTAD, author of *Entrepreneurial Faith, A Passionate Life, The Passionate Church*, and *Turn Your Church Inside Out*, and senior pastor of Community Church of Joy in Glendale, Arizona

"It's been said that all evil needs to succeed is for good men to do nothing. Kenny excels at showing the bigger story we're engaged in. *Fight* is a must read for men to defeat the enemy where *each of us* live—in our marriages, our families, and all our spheres of influence."

—JIM WEIDMANN, "The Family Night Guy," senior vice president of Promise Keepers, and author of the Family Night Tool Chest series

"I always want to know if the author of a book exemplifies what he has written. Kenny Luck certainly does!"

—TOM HOLLADAY, teaching pastor at Saddleback Church and author of *Foundations: 11 Core Truths to Build Your Life On*

"As a pastor, I get the joy of seeing how Kenny's message lives out weekly through our men at Saddleback Church. It's not theory, but real! Kenny's passion and calling is making a difference!"

—DOUG SLAYBAUGH, president, Purpose Driven

fight

workbook

fight

workbook

Are you willing to pick a
Fight with Evil?

kenny luck

WATERBROOK
PRESS

Fight Workbook
Published by WaterBrook Press
12265 Oracle Boulevard, Suite 200
Colorado Springs, Colorado 80921
A division of Random House Inc.

All Scripture quotations, unless otherwise indicated, are taken from the Holy Bible, New International Version®. NIV®. Copyright © 1973, 1978, 1984 by International Bible Society. Used by permission of Zondervan Publishing House. All rights reserved. Scripture quotations marked (MSG) are taken from The Message by Eugene H. Peterson. Copyright © 1993, 1994, 1995, 1996, 2000, 2001, 2002. Used by permission of NavPress Publishing Group. All rights reserved. Scripture quotations marked (NASB) are taken from the New American Standard Bible®. © Copyright The Lockman Foundation 1960, 1962, 1963, 1968, 1971, 1972, 1973, 1975, 1977, 1995. Used by permission. (www.Lockman.org). Scripture quotations marked (NLT 1996) are taken from the Holy Bible, New Living Translation, copyright © 1996. Used by permission of Tyndale House Publishers Inc., Wheaton, Illinois 60189. All rights reserved.

Italics in Scripture quotations reflect the author's added emphasis.

ISBN 978-1-57856-993-9

Published in the United States by WaterBrook Multnomah, an imprint of The Doubleday Publishing Group, a division of Random House Inc., New York.

Printed in the United States of America
2008—First Edition

10 9 8 7 6 5 4 3 2 1

Most WaterBrook Multnomah books are available in special quantity discounts when purchased in bulk by corporations, organizations, and special interest groups. Custom imprinting or excerpting can also be done to fit special needs. For information, please e-mail SpecialMarkets@WaterBrookMultnomah.com or call 1-800-603-7051.

contents

how to use this workbook

This workbook companion to the book *Fight* is designed to be used in three ways:

1. *Personal workbook.* If you want to better understand the spiritual battle that is raging and how you can become a better-trained warrior who makes the Enemy quiver, you will profit greatly from a careful study of this material. Each session in the workbook contains two sections for personal study and action: Fight Intel and Fight Orders (including key scripture—Remember—to memorize during the week's study). If you read the assigned chapters in *Fight,* which I strongly recommend, plan on investing at least two hours on each lesson, as well as some dedicated time memorizing the short verses.

2. *One-on-one study* for you and an accountability partner. Find a brother (or two) interested in learning more about the tactics and strategies of the Devil to study with you. This is potentially the best way to get the most benefit from this workbook. Each week, both you and your reconnaissance buddy will do your individual study of the session material. Then you'll get together to discuss the content and work as a team on some questions in the Fight Reconnaissance sections.

3. *Small group discussion guide.* Imagine the friendships you could form by getting together to enjoy a shared interest like learning the art of tactical warfare against evil! There's nothing like sharing battle stories and real-life victories, and supporting each other in weekly prayer, to bond a small group together. Toward that end, each session of the *Fight Workbook* includes a list of questions in the Fight Small Unit Tactics section. These discussions will be most rewarding if every participant completes the personal workbook study before the small group meeting.

The end of each session includes the suggested readings and any suggested assignments for the week.

No matter how you use this workbook, you'll have abundant opportunities to learn a great deal about your spiritual fight and how to not only defend against Satan's attacks, but take the battle deep into his territory. Commit to participate in every element—personal workbook, one-on-one accountability, and small group discussion—and watch your fighting skills take off.

Finally, we've included space for you to write answers, comments, and questions—called the Fight Journal—following the conclusion of each session. Use this space to write any ideas, conclusions, challenges, or personal insights you find meaningful from that week's session.

This workbook is designed for eight, twelve, or sixteen weeks depending on your group's time commitment and size. Completing the study may take less or more time one-on-one or if you or your recon partner is currently struggling with deep spiritual issues. Above all, invest the time you need personally, despite what your group or partners require. It's not unusual for a group to spend two or three meetings completing one session. An important rule of thumb is to always go for *depth* over *distance*.

Before you begin your sessions, commit your time to God. Ask the Holy Spirit to illuminate His Word in your mind, guide your heart, and energize your spirit as you read each section and answer each question.

Don't be afraid to adapt this workbook so that it works for *you*. This is your workbook, your invitation to know God and His ways better, to learn about the spiritual war going on inside and around you, and to become an effective battler for the king-dom of God. So, toward that end, dedicate yourself to the task at hand, and watch your commitment manifest in your increased spiritual strength.

Got it, God's man? It's time to *fight*.

introduction

This is not your average spiritual warfare workbook. In fact, this one could save your life.

Does that sound melodramatic? Maybe going a bit too far?

As it relates to your preparedness for this business of daily Christian living, and as it concerns your overall spiritual health and well-being, I doubt I could overstate the importance of this workbook's information, as well as our more-complete discussion on the struggle against evil in the third God's man book, *Fight*.

The reason is that at this very moment, a war is being fought to the death between good and evil, and it's happening all around us and even inside us. And it never stops. Don't believe me? Turn on the evening news. Talk to a single mom whose husband has left her because he didn't love her anymore. Look at the stats on aborted children, rape victims, suicides, and teens hooked on meth. Deranged shooters taking on schools, ministries, and churches. Elders and pastors whose porn habits are destroying their ministries and families.

Brother, bullets are flying.

At the start, however, I need to warn you that Satan doesn't like you being here. In fact, he hates it, and as you begin to study his personality, his deceptions, and the ways of his colaborers in evil, you too will earn his rage and go on his Most Wanted list. I don't say this to scare you—but you need to be aware. You'll need to gain certain disciplines and be alert to his tactics that pressure you to quit. After all, our enemy is on the prowl, a "roaring lion" looking for a quick meal, according to the apostle Peter.

While writing *Fight,* I got familiar with that lion's putrid breath. The Devil prowled and growled over my relationships, my work, my travel plans, and my writing schedule. He tried to intimidate me with bizarre events and evil presences, and even planted horrible accusations in my mind the night before a speaking engagement.

Jesus nailed it when He said that Satan's game is "to steal and kill and destroy" (John 10:10). When you love, follow, and obey Jesus, you are always in the sights of the Devil's rifle scope. And when you start learning more about taking the battle to him, his eye will be on you, his finger on the trigger. So watch and be ready, God's man.

Jesus came to earth "to destroy the devil's work" (1 John 3:8), and I made that my mission as well in this book and workbook—to share my gut about making war on evil. If you'll dedicate yourself to finding out what's required to be an effective warrior for Christ and to using your weapons well, your life will not be in danger. But fail to believe in and understand the deeper spiritual conflict we're all in, and you *will* most certainly die on the battlefield. The kingdom tasks God intended for you will fall to another.

If you can avoid it, don't attempt to study this workbook alone. I strongly recommend that you find at least one like-minded soldier who will walk through this material with you. In the body of Christ, there's definitely strength in numbers. As the battle rages, your brothers can lay down some covering fire for you. Find a buddy—better yet, start or join a *Fight* small group. That's the best way to ensure you'll have the support and commitment this is going to take.

So if you're good with all that, welcome to the fight, brother! I'm counting on you. We need each other. And in Jesus' strength and the power of His name, we will prevail!

bring it on!

This week's session is based on chapter 1, "Ignorance Is Incompetence," and chapter 2, "The Nonfiction Demon," in Fight.

Are you looking for a fight?

Whether you accept it or not, if you call yourself a follower of Jesus Christ, you're in a knockdown, drag-out brawl with evil, both in the flesh you no longer claim and in the culture around you. Another term for this ubiquitous struggle is *the Christian life.*

Yet unfortunately, too many of God's men seem not to *know* or even *care* that they are in this fight, and this attitude guarantees heavy losses and, potentially, spiritual defeat for themselves and those around them.

The first step toward repairing this pervasive problem must come in accepting—versus denying—our roles in the larger spiritual battle. As we learned in *Fight,* Jesus never ran from the struggle: "The reason the Son of God appeared was to destroy the devil's work" (1 John 3:8). Standing in His strength, we must say as a team, *"Bring it on!"*

But there can be no doubt—our enemy is clever and ruthless. Remember, passion is not enough. We must prepare. This companion workbook has been intentionally constructed to equip you to defend against the Devil's schemes and take the battle deep into his territory.

 ## Fight Intel

📖 Most believers are aware of the "right answers" when it comes to the familiar idea of waging spiritual warfare. And yet we're failing at practical application. We look at the cosmic conflict between good and evil more like a Harry Potter movie—it's a tossup which side will prevail until the final frame. And it's this perspective when applied to the *real world* of spiritual attack that breeds insecurity, hesitation, vacillation, and harm to both believer and the cause of Christ...

We will have struck a deep blow to our enemy if our concept of the spiritual battle moves forcefully from being an afterthought to a way to believe and behave. Based on the attitudes I encounter in men worldwide regarding evil, *I would want us for an opponent if I were Satan.* The painful, sad reality is that the underworld has the upper hand on the ground level of this war with God's men. 📖

1. Why do you think many Christians are hesitant to discuss the reality of our spiritual fight with evil?

2. Do your responses to evil in your everyday life match your belief in the real world of spiritual attack?

📖 When it comes to being God's man, discipleship and discomfort are very closely connected.

Being with Jesus in the first century meant regular discussions about Satan and engaging evil forces. Imagine: for the disciples, being with Jesus was for the specific intention of gaining the authority and training to cast out demons! The Gospels, the book of Acts, the pastoral epistles, and John's vision in Revelation all talk about evil making its play in the life of the believers. The norm for a New Testament God's man is to regularly recognize and deal with evil.

Today this kind of fearlessness is completely absent. Spiritual warfare is considered too "out there," misinformation, or someone else's calling. The Bible calls Satan "the ruler of this world." Thinking wrongly about him, or not at all, gives him his greatest tactical advantage. 📖

3. Review the encounter Jesus had with the Devil in the wilderness (see Luke 4:1–13). Based on this incident, list any impressions you have of Satan's character and his tactics.

4. Why would "thinking wrongly…or not at all" about Satan turn out to be Satan's greatest tactical advantage?

📖 Satan knows who you are.… He doesn't play fair and is the king of low blows.… Magnifying emotions to create insecurities, heighten fears, and defeat us without a bullet being shot are the things Satan is best at. He must rely on playing mind games—a sign of insecurity and no real power.… He is doing the same thing with you *right now.* 📖

5. Satan is described in Scripture as a deceiver (see Revelation 12:9). In your own experience, how have you been deceived by Satan and other evil influences?

6. As you begin this workbook, what opposition from the Enemy have you already encountered?

📖 It's time to look in the mirror and not be satisfied with what we have become in the midst of the great war for our King. We must make peace with the fact that we are spiritually enabled, empowered, and equipped to make war on the Enemy and *do something*. We are commissioned to inflict losses, unmask and thwart plots to kill, and deliver those in bondage to darkness into the freedom of the sons of light. 📖

7. Paraphrase Kenny's statement above and apply it to your own life.

Prepare to FIGHT

How should we prepare to become elite warriors in the raging battle between good and evil?

📖 Your attitude about evil reflects your stand against evil…. The great men of faith understood this, and as God's man, so must you. To help you with this, we need to think about evil and our fight with it in uncomplicated terms that are consistent with Scripture and practical to apply. We need to think better before we can fight better. The "We've got Jesus, yes we do. We've got Jesus, how about you?" approach is as effective as it sounds. The Bible does not support it, though it might work at Vacation Bible School. In fact, the more emotional you are in warfare, the sooner you die. So in the interest of living to fight another day, let's replace emotional and unsuccessful strategies with intelligent and intentional ways of thinking about and fighting evil. 📖

1. Why will your attitude about evil reflect your actions against evil?

2. In the past, how intelligent and intentional have your strategies been against evil? Explain your answer.

In *Fight,* the five principles that change our attitude and our personal stand against evil are

> **F**ace the Reality of Evil
> **I**ntegrate Intel on the Enemy
> **G**row Progressively More Aware of Evil
> **H**andle Your Weapons with Consistency and Confidence
> **T**ake the Fight to Evil

Throughout the *Fight Workbook,* you will be encouraged to apply each of these principles in deeper and stronger ways. Let's take a closer look at them now.

Face the Reality of Evil

Satan unequivocally wants you dead or at least neutralized (living but not a threat). For God's man the most tragic mistake you can make is to sort of believe in evil, its existence, and its specific designs on your life. When God's men approach the reality of evil this way, we send a clear message to our enemy. What we are saying is that intellectually and mentally we believe there is an evil ringleader guiding plots against us, but practically, we act as though he has nothing to do with what befalls us. We behave like all our problems have natural causes and solutions; none have supernatural causes and divine solutions. We end up responding to problems that require supernatural responses with human wisdom and natural solutions. We are firing water pistols at an armed destroyer.

3. How would you describe your own belief in Satan's influence in your daily affairs? Are you:

_____ not very conscious of his involvement?

_____ moderately conscious of his involvement?

_____ extremely conscious of his involvement?

4. Give some reasons why you chose this answer.

While we may not be disbelievers in evil or overbelievers (where the Devil is behind everything bad that happens), functionally we are sort-of believers, and God's men are getting killed.... Face it: Satan has been watching film on you.

He's relentless. Get that one firmly planted in your brain. Even *after* getting taken to the shed by the Son of God, the Bible says that "he left him *until the next opportunity came*" (Luke 4:13, NLT 2004). Satan is not just relentless but a relentless opportunist. He *never* rests. 📖

5. Have you been a "sort-of" believer in evil? Do you have difficulty discerning when Satan is taking an opportunity to damage your walk with Christ? Explore the reasons for your answer and commit yourself to integrating more intel on his deceptions.

Integrate Intel on the Enemy

Reliable information on the Enemy is critical to successful warfare.

📖 In helping the Corinthians, the apostle Paul acted just like [a] spiritual counterterrorism expert.... As he gathered information about all the conflicts among believers over various issues, he saw an emerging pattern and trend as he analyzed the data. Lo and behold, the fingerprints of the Evil One were popping up in his mental database....

"The reason I wrote you was to see if you would stand the test and be obedient in everything. If you forgive anyone, I also forgive him. And what I have forgiven—if there was anything to forgive—I have forgiven in the sight of Christ for your sake, *in order that Satan might not outwit us. For we are not unaware of his schemes*" (2 Corinthians 2:9–11).

Translation: Based on the intel, we know who's *really* behind this and we're going to take the necessary steps (join in forgiving people) to stop this terrorist threat. The sledgehammer application is this: If you are *unaware*, you will be *outwitted* by evil. If you are outwitted, people around you get hurt, and the cause of the kingdom suffers. The reverse scenario is equally valid. If you are actively integrating your intelligence and matrixing that intel with what you know to be true about how evil operates, you will preempt and shut down the Devil's terrorist schemes against you, other believers, the church, and the world. 📖

6. Can you think of a past situation in your life where your unawareness of Satan's schemes ended up causing harm?

7. Has there been a situation where your understanding of Satan's schemes prevented disaster?

Grow Progressively More Aware of Evil

📖 "Keep a cool head. Stay alert. The Devil is poised to pounce, and would like nothing better than to catch you napping. Keep your guard up" (1 Peter 5:8–9, MSG). Heady. Alert. Guard up. Any other attitude toward the active and present threat of evil is, by default, suicidal. This might be termed an aggressive aware-ness based on the recognition of reality. When you are not awake and aware, you are asleep and vulnerable. A reactive strategy usually means you're too late. Too late means you find fangs in the back of your neck....

Gen. Douglas MacArthur had a propensity for noting the obvious when it came to fighting wars, winning battles, and avoiding defeats. D. Mac's wisdom is telling for every God's man. "The history of failure in war can almost be summed up in two words, too late. Too late in comprehending the deadly pur-pose of a potential enemy. Too late in realizing mortal danger. Too late in pre-paredness. Too late in uniting all possible forces for resistance. Too late in standing with one's friends." 📖

8. What specific areas of your life stand out to you as needing more alertness to the threats of the Devil?

Handle Your Weapons with Consistency and Confidence

📖 Jesus is our ultimate trainer in the art of spiritual battle. His weapons are our weapons, passed through the ages to men of faith. The goal is to handle them skillfully. Versus what? Versus clumsily and incompetently. In our hearts we know confidently understanding our arsenal will mean a confident mental-ity and stance under fire. With a real, supernatural showdown looming with a highly trained enemy, only arrogance and stupidity would cause a God's man to reach for self-prescribed wisdom and solutions. "We are human, but we don't wage war with human plans and methods. We use God's mighty weapons, not mere worldly weapons, to knock down the Devil's strongholds" (2 Corinthians 10:3–4, NLT 1996).

The weapons God has supplied are to be *used* against evil. Not just used before meals, when calamities strike, or to make your life more comfortable and pain free....

Only use and familiarity make you dangerous with a weapon. 📖

9. In what circumstances or situations are you more comfortable using your spiritual weapons to do battle? When are you less comfortable?

Take the Fight to Evil

📖 You are about to embark on the greatest crusade known to men and angels. Heaven is watching, and the hopes and prayers of your brothers march with you. Locking arms with other brave soldiers in Christ serving on other fronts, you will be called to bring about the destruction of evil plots against the good, the elimination of the stranglehold of Satan over the lives of others, and the advancement of the kingdom of God.

This undertaking will not be trouble free or painless. Your enemy is intelligent, skilled, and personally driven by his cause. He will fight viciously. But God's Spirit declares this is a new day for men He is making new. The tide is turning, and the days of living in defeat and despair have been replaced with the full commitment of God's men who are willing to fight in the open, hand to hand. Our collective focus on exposing, isolating, and moving aggressively against evil will change and reduce evil's capacity to wage war. We have overwhelmingly superior weaponry placed at our disposal and rising numbers of skilled warriors locking arms. God's men are on the march, and we are resolved to accept nothing less than a full victory, even if that means our very lives. 📖

10. Why is our fight against evil on earth a great crusade?

11. What troubles you—if anything—about the fight against evil?

Recap: The five categories of training and tactical abilities you will gain from this workbook are

> **F**acing the reality of evil head on
> **I**ntegrating the intelligence God has provided in Scripture
> **G**rowing progressively more aware of Satan's presence
> **H**andling your weapons with skill and dangerous intention
> **T**aking the fight to the Enemy.

📖 God has full confidence in your loyalty to His cause and your abilities to fight for Him when you are called upon by circumstances and the commission of Christ. Your King has declared to you, *"All authority in heaven and on earth has been given to me"* (Matthew 28:18). It's time we get that and deal with evil the right way—expose it, engage it, and keep it on the run *through* Christ. 📖

 **Fight Drill**

As you complete the Fight Intel sections, I'll have you spend a few minutes summarizing what we have covered. An absolutely crucial aspect of being effective in the spiritual fight is knowing what God says about various issues. We also look to Him for the power to wage the good fight. I urge you to memorize an important *Fight* verse in each session, which will always be highlighted here under the Remember heading.

Remember

The reason the Son of God appeared was to destroy the devil's work. (1 John 3:8)

Reflect

1. What work of the Devil did Jesus come to destroy?

2. As you look at the categories of the fight (above), which topics seem most relevant to you now? What do you need to learn most through this training workbook?

Respond

As you begin to face the reality of the spiritual fight, list the overall goals you want to achieve.

 Fight Reconnaissance (Man to Man)

Warning: You must not think that your fight against Satan and evil is something you should do by yourself. Yes, much spiritual battle is conducted individually in hand-to-hand combat with the Enemy, but you must always operate as part of a unit of like-minded men. A great place to build your defenses and discuss intelligence about the

Enemy, gathered via reconnaissance, is in a one-to-one accountability relationship with a fellow brother. In each session, I'll list several questions for you to ask each other—ideally at a time when you get together each week to find out how the battle is going, to fill up on the truth of the Word, and to pray.

Ask each other these questions:

1. Up to now, what ideas have you had about the spiritual battle? Were you interested or not in your personal role in the fight?
2. What are some specific things you want to learn about your individual spiritual fight?
3. Share personal needs and requests and pray for each other.

 ## Fight Small Unit Tactics (Small Group Discussion)

1. What are some reasons the topic of spiritual warfare is often a controversial topic in the Christian community?
2. What reactions concerning our involvement in the spiritual fight have you encountered among the Christians you know?
3. How does it make you feel that your sworn enemy, the Devil, has as his mission—related to you—to "steal and kill and destroy" (John 10:10)?
4. What evidence do you see of Satan's vicious war in your own experience and in your relationships with others?
5. Jesus said, "All authority in heaven and on earth has been given to me" (Matthew 28:18). How should this statement by Jesus influence our approach to Satan and evil?
6. Kenny writes, "What we need are God's men who are not apathetic, ambivalent, or indifferent to evil. We can no longer afford to stand idly by and give Satan

permission to abuse our brothers and sisters. We must face the reality of evil to stop the two things that most embolden and accelerate Satan's campaigns: the incompetence and passivity of Christ's followers." How can we as Christian men move from being passive about evil to a more aggressive, proactive response?

7. We must not forget the second part of John 10:10, which reads, "I [Jesus] have come that they may have life, and have it to the full." Based on this statement by Jesus, what kind of outcome should we expect as we confront the Devil and evil?

 ## Fight Orders

Here's what needs to happen before the next small group meeting:

1. Complete your personal study of session 2, which includes reading chapters 3 and 4 in *Fight*.
2. Meet with your reconnaissance (accountability) partner.
3. Complete the Fight Drill section of chapter 1 on page 19.
4. Record your ideas and personal reflections in the Fight Journal.

 ## Fight Journal

_____

_____

_____

expose the darkness

This week's session is based on chapter 3, "Passion Is Not Enough," and chapter 4, "That One Thing," in Fight.

Jesus got really angry one day at some men who were looking good on the outside but must have had some major stink on the inside: "Woe to you, teachers of the law and Pharisees, you hypocrites! You are like whitewashed tombs, which look beautiful on the outside but on the inside are full of dead men's bones and everything unclean" (Matthew 23:27).

Nothing has changed since Jesus laid the wood on those guys. We can't expect to do much damage against evil if our hearts are landfills of bad attitudes, anger, unforgiveness, fear, lust, selfishness, or greed. We must get clean ourselves before we can go clean up the evil messes of this world. Here's where we start getting that done.

 Fight Intel

📖 It seems almost every week I hear of another leader or fellow pastor in God's army who has been shot down after what seemed to be an awesome beginning....

For these men and others like them, their sin did not bring about their fall; it was their *lack of discernment and understanding of their foe.* Somewhere along the way God's man

- compartmentalized the evil
- made the Enemy an abstract theological construct
- ignored God's warnings
- and never saw the Devil coming.

Satan fired the shots, but *ignorance* was the real culprit....

Satan is legendary for his ability to take down the best of men who began their journey with Christ fully equipped with all the resources of God and the best of intentions. Get that. *We have to see just how good he is at this in order to raise our respect and awareness to where it needs to be.* While ownership of the spiritual resources for our dogfight with evil is guaranteed, that does not mean possession of or mastery over or victory in our fight on earth. Zeal and equipment are not enough. 📖

1. When taking on Satan in warfare over some personal character weakness or some evil in our environment, why are zeal and equipment not enough to win a battle?

2. From what you've heard or read or experienced in your life, why do you think men who are Christian leaders seem so morally vulnerable to Satan's temptations?

Warfare Training with Jesus

After Jesus had spent some time training His men, this is what He told them about the larger kingdom picture:

📖 "The harvest is plentiful but the workers are few. Ask the Lord of the harvest, therefore, to send out workers into his harvest field" (Matthew 9:37)....

This whole time they were learning the art of war, how to advance the kingdom amid hostile men of all persuasions—religious, political, cultural, and satanic. He was showing them how a compassionate God's man fights during his time on earth: teaching, preaching, healing, and boldly liberating those who are held captive and controlled by the god of this world and by sin....

He called His twelve disciples to Him and "gave them authority to drive out evil spirits and to heal every disease and sickness." He told them, "As you go, preach this message: 'The kingdom of heaven is near.' Heal the sick, raise the dead, cleanse those who have leprosy, drive out demons. Freely you have received, freely give.... I am sending you out like sheep among wolves. Therefore be as shrewd as snakes and as innocent as doves" (Matthew 10:1, 7–8, 16). 📖

1. Before this study, had you thought of "teaching, preaching, healing, and boldly liberating those who are held captive" as part of the spiritual fight? Do you see how this applies in your own life?

2. In your life, what do you think it means to be a worker in Jesus' harvest field?

📖 With the full endorsement of the Supreme Commander, God's men were given
- a sanction to fight ("gave them authority")
- a message to forward ("preach this")
- targets to find (sick, dead, lepers, demon possessed)
- power to free (to heal, raise, cleanse, and drive out)
- a charge to feel ("freely you have received, freely give")
- a metaphor to familiarize ("sending you out like sheep among wolves")
- two commands to fulfill ("be shrewd" and "innocent")

Jesus didn't provide false hope or codependent comfort. He gave it to them straight—this was the campaign to rid the world of Satan's grip through kingdom advance. 📖

3. What evidence of Satan's grip do you see in your workplace? in your community? in the media? in your church? in your family? in you?

Jesus commanded His disciples, in the midst of the wolves, to "be as shrewd as snakes and as innocent as doves."

📖 When you think "shrewd," you think *perceptive* and *not naive*. Perfect preparation before going into war. In other words, "Be clear about your mission, be intentional, and don't compromise it by getting lazy—or else." The same command is now put to you, God's man, as we prepare to go forward into the fight. 📖

4. What do you think "be as shrewd as snakes and as innocent as doves" means?

📖 An innocent God's man will
- seek to keep his heart clean before God so he can hear His voice
- openly examine himself before God *and* man—no secrets
- hate evil and run from it if necessary to preserve his integrity
- control himself to keep polluting influences out of his relationship with God
- become increasingly unsullied by his old ways of living
- put strong boundaries in his life to preempt evil assaults
- control his thoughts and not allow any that are outside the will of God
- soak his mind in God's thoughts and desires
- seek aggressive accountability and use it to win his battles with evil

Jesus knew that innocence to evil and sin was the secret to clarity of mind and receptivity to His Spirit in battle. 📖

5. Why is innocence such a source of strength in successfully combating the Enemy's tactics?

📖 Jesus is intentional with His men as He prepares them for war. He calls them to wisdom before warfare and virtue before victory.... He also desired His fighters to *actively defer to and be directed by* divine wisdom and realities over their own. He prayed over us, "Sanctify them by the truth; your word is truth" (John 17:17). A spiritually shrewd man is a man of the Word. 📖

6. Why is knowledge of scriptural truth important in fighting the spiritual war?

📖 God's man can unwittingly, unknowingly, or ignorantly partner with the Devil.... For this reason, we can't go freewheeling into the topics of and training for spiritual battle without first dealing with the guy in the mirror. 📖

The Rock

Some incidents in the life of Peter provide an illustration of how each of us is influenced by Satan's tricks and our own sinfulness.

Take a closer look and consider that even Peter the Rock was blind to the darkness in him.... Lurking just beneath the surface of Peter's award-winning commitment to Christ was *that one thing.... That one thing*, that aspect of Peter that would get in the way of all that passion, commitment, and energy, was leaking and visible. In Luke 22, we see it come out, and Jesus addresses it in a weird and ominous way. All God's men who will fight evil must pause and reflect on how our Commander feels about character preceding influence....

"Simon, Simon, Satan has asked to have all of you, to sift you like wheat. But I have pleaded in prayer for you, Simon, that your faith should not fail. So when you have repented and turned to me again, strengthen and build up your brothers." Peter said, "Lord I am ready to go to prison with you, and even to die with you" (Luke 22:25–33, NLT 1996).

Praying for me against Satan? When I repent and turn back to Him? Peter's stomach must have clenched up real tight, his mind must have started racing, his defenses and insecurities skyrocketing to Code Red. This is the definition of an awkward moment. "Uh, sorry, Jesus. I was just staking my claim." At this point, Peter was the most high-profile disciple on the team. He'd just been guaranteed a starring role in eternity. And just as they're sharing this intimate moment, *THWACK!* Jesus pours water on the "Rock-star." We now know who's going to be the greatest by whom Satan is asking to sift.... A few long seconds pass. Peter's brain is crunching the data. Then his response, "Fine. Bring it on. I'll prove I'm all that." Predictably proud, ambitious, and self-sufficient, Peter can't help himself. Whether it's the awkwardness of the moment, his false sense of self, or ignorance about just how severe his sifting process would be, *that one thing* leaks out. 📖

1. How precisely did Peter's one thing trip him up? In your own words, what was Jesus' response?

2. Does your one thing cause you to struggle? How have you been handling it up to now?

📖 He'd be used by God in all the ways Jesus promised, but only *after* the sifting, *after* the purification of his character.... Sifting is synonymous with elimination. What Peter could not recognize in *himself*, God eliminated. He allowed Peter to be selected and exposed to a trial and testing that would *separate* and *eliminate* his ego from his service for Christ, deconstruct the old Peter, and raise up a new man with a new *character*. There is no longer a place for darkness to dwell in his life. It has been replaced with the light of the character of Christ Himself—an impenetrable force. 📖

The New Testament records that the sifting process in Peter's life was a success. This rough fisherman went on to be a key leader in the early church and wrote letters later included in the New Testament.

> We each have a key task to complete before we set out to fight evil: discerning the darkness in our own hearts. Jesus said, "Make sure that the light *you think you have* is not really darkness. If you are filled with light, *with no dark corners,* then your whole life will be radiant, as though a floodlight were filling you with light" (Luke 11:35–36, NLT 1996).... He knew this one thing would be critical for His followers: the strange dynamic of how faith gets hijacked by evil. It's a terrifying thought, Jesus' telling us we'll have to actively evaluate ourselves to keep from becoming an unwitting pawn for evil. But if it's true that Christians can be doing God's work, shining His light, *and simultaneously* be providing a safe haven for darkness, we have some heart investigation to do.

3. What are some dark corners that men seem more likely to struggle with?

4. What are some things a man can do to shed light on dark corners in his life?

📖 An attitude, an action, a way of thinking, or a way of living are all possible places of moral darkness *and*... a place where Satan is free to traffic, transport, and transact evil. Unfortunately, most believers compartmentalize this truth and believe this darkness is a place *beyond* them in some other realm. No. He is bound to be wherever darkness abides....

Pastor Francis Frangipane understands the confusion most Christians face over Satan's presence, but he doesn't protect us from the cold, hard fact about Satan's freedom to set up shop in any dark space: "Many Christians debate whether the devil is on earth or in hell; can he dwell in Christians or only in the world? The fact is, the devil is in the darkness. Wherever there is spiritual darkness, there the devil will be." 📖

5. Do you agree or disagree that Satan is bound to be wherever darkness abides? List reasons for your answer.

Target the Internal Darkness

📖 When you harbor sin, you become a courier for darkness, and God will not entrust the kingdom fight or work to such a man. Instead, you will get worked.... What's going on inside of you? *That* is more critical to victory in the bigger fight than whatever words you're saying. Look at Peter, and then look at yourself. If you want to become an easy mark for Satan, simply deny, excuse, or rationalize this. But if you want to play a key part in the battle, consider the dark footholds of sin, pride, or fear you're having trouble letting go of

- an arrogant or self-centered spirit
- a growing materialistic tendency
- overconcern with titles, status, or position
- an addiction to approval
- a secret sexual sin
- an overreaction to criticism
- emotional reliance upon past successes
- closemindedness or an unteachable spirit
- an unwillingness to be accountable to others
- a disregard for core spiritual disciplines
- a disconnectedness from your spouse
- behaviors that isolate you from other Christians
- harbored resentments or unforgiveness
- a critical spirit
- discontentment, jealousy, or envy
- defensiveness
- disrespect of others
- an attitude of entitlement and lack of humility
- permitting questionable behaviors

All of these are examples of *that one thing* with one common denominator: dangerous darkness of character. 📖

1. Why is "what's going on inside of you" so critical to achieving growth and victory in the Christian life?

2. Concerning the bulleted list above, circle the items that represent areas of darkness in your life. In prayer, ask the Lord to reveal how He wants you to respond to each circled issue—for example, repent, seek forgiveness, ask for wise counsel, change behavior, and so on. This is the time for a good internal power wash!

📖 It's when God's man *assimilates the character of Christ* in a dark area that the Devil withdraws.... In times of sifting, a fighting faith is produced, pure and unassailable. And if you respond decisively, Satan will be forced to abandon his sabotage as Christ's own nature in you successfully walls off those dark aspects of your inner construction. 📖

3. Do you recall times when you were sifted? Write down some of the understanding you gained during such siftings.

📖 Of deep delight to God is when a believer cooperates with Him in knocking sin, pride, and presumption down on a regular basis and keeps darkness on the run....

The result? God can then entrust you with the weightier responsibilities of His kingdom. In the kingdom's theaters of spiritual battle, the men who get deployed to the battle lines *out there* have already dealt with the terrorist cell *in here* (tap your chest for me). Go after *that one thing.* 📖

4. Have you been going after that one thing in your own life consistently and intentionally?

 **Fight Drill**

Remember

Make sure that the light you think you have is not really darkness. If you are filled with light, with no dark corners, then your whole life will be radiant, as though a floodlight is filling you with light. (Luke 11:35–36, NLT 1996)

Reflect

1. Is there anything in your life that looks like light but really is more like darkness?

2. In prayer ask the Lord to forgive you of any areas of darkness and sin in your interior life. Joyfully receive His forgiveness (see 1 John 1:9) and walk boldly forward knowing that you are clean (see Hebrews 9:14)!

Respond

During this next week, on a daily basis, take five minutes and do a self-inventory by asking this question: What areas of darkness in my interior life need Christ's exposing and purifying light today? Repent, seek forgiveness, be filled with the Holy Spirit, and move on.

 Fight Reconnaissance (Man to Man)

Take turns asking each other these questions:

1. How has this last week been for you—what evidence of a deeper spiritual struggle have you seen in your life?
2. How difficult is it for you to admit your weaknesses—the areas of darkness you struggle with?
3. Pray for one another about your areas of need—and any other requests you may have.

 ## Fight Small Unit Tactics (Small Group Discussion)

1. In *Fight* we read, "Take this in, God's man: You are a sheep among wolves *right now.* One of the main reasons we are getting massacred is that we are sheep among wolves, but we act like sheep among squirrels." What does Kenny mean when he says that Christian men "act like sheep among squirrels"?
2. In accepting the reality of spiritual assault, it's important that we be shrewd in understanding the Enemy. In your experience, what are some of Satan's tactics that he uses to defeat us?
3. One of Satan's top strategies is to hide his evil intentions behind a masquerade of light. Can you list some examples of this tactic?
4. Kenny writes, "When you harbor sin, you become a courier for darkness, and God will not entrust the kingdom fight or work to such a man. Instead, you will get worked." Why is the harboring of sin so destructive to your spiritual life?
5. In what areas should we as men become increasingly innocent?
6. When God wants to more deeply purify our hearts, He may choose sifting as His instrument of change. Have you been sifted by God? Share what that was like and the results.
7. Read what the apostle Paul wrote to Timothy below. What noble purposes might God have in mind for the man who cleanses himself?

In a large house there are articles not only of gold and silver, but also of wood and clay; some are for noble purposes and some for ignoble. If a man cleanses himself from the latter, he will be an instrument for noble purposes, made holy, useful to the Master and prepared to do any good work. (2 Timothy 2:20–21)

8. What purposes do you think God might have waiting for you if you will cleanse yourself and seek to serve Him in obedience?

 Fight Orders

Here's what needs to happen before the next small group meeting:

1. Complete your personal study of session 3, which includes reading chapters 6 and 7 in *Fight*.
2. Meet with your accountability partner.
3. Complete the Fight Drill section on page 37.
4. Record your observations in the Fight Journal.

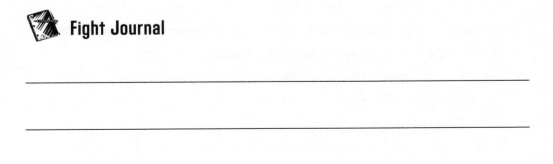 **Fight Journal**

_____

_____

_____

satan's résumé

This week's session is based on chapter 6, "The Arsonist: Part One," and chapter 7, "The Arsonist: Part Two," in Fight.

Many people seem to fall into two extreme camps when dealing with Satan. On the one hand, some Christians are very focused on the Devil. Almost everything that happens to them is linked to the Devil's extreme interest in fouling up their lives. At the other extreme, no doubt the more dangerous position, are the Christians who hardly acknowledge that Satan exists.

The best approach is to understand all we can about Satan so we can engage his tactics in quick and effective ways to "bring the troops home" (both believers and unbelievers). Satan is a vicious foe, but we have true power over evil. Let's look at what we need to know about public enemy number one.

 Fight Intel

📖 The Bible contains the file on Satan. In it we find what we need to know about him, his history, his failures, his abilities, his plans, and his intentions toward us. The first step in discerning evil is to understand that Satan is a living personality with a complex depth of character. He has an inner life that informs his actions and shapes his existence. He also has a past. To discern him, we must get intimate with his personality and how it was formed. He certainly has a reputation, but that comes from his character.

What formed his character is right there in his file. As with [arsonist John] Orr's rejection after a failed psychological exam, there was something inside Satan that God's holiness couldn't accept. Something wasn't right. There was a flaw, an unhealthy fondness for the power of his position, that turned him self-serving. God sensed it and responded in a manner consistent with His character, banishing Satan from heaven:

> You were anointed as a guardian cherub,
>> for so I ordained you.
> You were on the holy mount of God;
>> you walked among the fiery stones.
> You were blameless in your ways
>> from the day you were created
>> till wickedness was found in you.
> Through your widespread trade
>> you were filled with violence,
>> and you sinned.
> So I drove you in disgrace from the mount of God,
>> and I expelled you, O guardian cherub,
>> from among the fiery stones.
> Your heart became proud
>> on account of your beauty,
> and you corrupted your wisdom
>> because of your splendor.

So I threw you to the earth;

    I made a spectacle of you before kings.

By your many sins and dishonest trade

    you have desecrated your sanctuaries.

So I made a fire come out from you,

    and it consumed you,

and I reduced you to ashes on the ground

    in the sight of all who were watching. (Ezekiel 28:14–18)

Satan was created by God and employed in His service. He stood between God and the praise that was offered. His merchandise was worship. Passing through his hands were the authority and dominion of God above him and the returned worship of created beings below him. He was a trusted employee, a senior manager, and the most articulate spokesman ever created. Then he *attached*.

He attached to himself some of the worship he was supposed to pass along to God. He attached to himself some of the authority that belonged to God alone. He attached to himself the orders God was giving and hijacked them, wanting some of his own under his own authority. He grew attached to his beauty, magnificence, and power and felt entitled to receive a little adulation for himself. Satan decided to embezzle God's glory. 📖

1. Among the different people you know, what terms would they use in describing Satan?

2. Using the quotation from Ezekiel above, what terms would you select that describe Satan?

3. What do you think might be the most common misperception of Satan?

📖 Satan was permanently banned from the job he loved, cast out and sent to a dark, formless, and vacuous earth void of life.... He was master of nothing, with lots of time for his anger to fester. 📖

4. What are the primary character qualities and emotions that Satan is known for?

📖 You and I are living in the next act of this unfolding story. In creating man, God gave Satan an object on which to project his latent hostility toward God.

The sufferings and agonies that have flowed from that moment lead us to the ultimate question we must resolve: *Why didn't God deal with Satan before allowing him to set the world on fire and create so much pain?* If you're like me, you can't look at the Holocaust, the genocide in Rwanda, 9/11, or myriad other senseless evils throughout history and *not* ask this question. And if you're like me, you might have a hard time getting your arms around the answer.... The reason I bring this up in our discussion of discerning evil and the need to understand Satan intimately is this: *you are his replacement.* You must get this. Not only does he know this, he loathes this with every fiber of his being. He loathes *you.* 📖

5. Are you surprised to learn that you and I took Satan's place in the heart of God? How does this truth adjust your understanding of Satan and his tactics?

6. Do you have a satisfactory answer as to why there's so much pain and suffering in the world?

Opening the Intel Files

📖 Pinning Satan is easier than catching a serial arsonist. He leaves the clean prints of his character and presence wherever he's been. So why, after Jesus' powerful work at the cross, the sending and indwelling of the Holy Spirit, the clear teaching about him by Jesus and Scripture, and the rapid spread of the gospel worldwide, have Satan's victories over God's people enjoyed such an incredible run? The first part of the answer has to do with Satan's potent skills. He's the master of redirecting suspicions about the points of origin and the person of origin *away from himself* and onto others, onto circumstances, onto organizations, churches, bad doctrine, anything else but the *real* source. The second part of the answer lies with us and our indifference toward his person, abilities, and designs upon us. Indifference is synonymous with ignorance, and ignorance is synonymous with defeat. That's why he's embarrassingly successful against God's people—functional knowledge undiligently applied. 📖

1. In your life experience, list some examples of incidents that reveal the cleverness of Satan.

2. Why do you think there's so much ignorance, even among Christians, about Satan?

📖 He's played us all at one time or another, and he's relentless at exerting his influence in every way he can. In relationships, in morals, in spiritually illuminating moments, and in emotional experiences, he's always involved. The reason is that these are where he gains the most: in the basic transactions of your soul. But knowing this in advance diminishes the chances that he can play you or manipulate you. Of course, just knowing this isn't enough. You must know *him*—his character and the ways it manifests in his conduct. When you see certain dynamics happening in people or situations, those reflect particular clues about their source. To catch the Great Arsonist, the spiritually aware God's man must make the causal connections. 📖

3. In what ways do you see Satan influencing the attitudes and behavior of other people?

4. What about you—where do you catch Satan messing with you?

Satan's Personality

📖 I cannot stress enough how God's man must read the Word with a lens for both spiritual application and fortification against the Enemy. We have to study and analyze with care every mention and appearance of Satan as well as his victories and defeats detailed in Scripture. In the most sinister way, all his character qualities become the methods he uses to kill. Discerning *him* leads us to discern what he's doing. His behavior always reflects his character. So let's look at a few more synonyms for Satan. When you see these in your circumstances, you can bank on his involvement at every level.

[Satan is] synonymous with pride. The language of pride is "I know better." It has multiple forms including all types of narcissism, self-promotion, defensiveness, arrogance, and entitlement. All of these separate people from God because they make people their own god, violating the first commandment and estranging them from their Creator. 📖

1. Why is pride such a source of interior darkness in people?

📖 *[Satan is] synonymous with death.* He is the original serial killer, and he is after more than stopping hearts. If homicide, suicide, or killing children is out of reach or ineffective, he will work to kill relationships, marriages, and families so that they will wipe out the next generation without more effort on his part. Abortion, yes, but divorce is just as good. 📖

2. What specific "deaths" have you seen in children, husbands, wives, and friends when Satan got involved in wrecking relationships?

📖 *Satan is synonymous with rebellion.* He's a rebel with a cause.... Rebellion is the name of Satan's game. 📖

3. Why is our wanting a high degree of control over other people and circumstances a sign of rebellion?

📖 *[Satan] is synonymous with out-of-control appetites.* Lives ruled by a fix, a meal, an adrenaline hit, a relationship, a purchase, a bet, a business deal, a porn site, or another immediate pleasure are easy to manage and destroy. 📖

4. Why do even harmless appetites or desires for food, coffee, or watching movies or following football on TV provide an environment for satanic influence?

📖 *Satan is synonymous with relational separation.* Satan is a lonely creature, has no friends, and is completely devoid of love. So he projects his own loneliness and misery upon people by attacking their connections to God and others. *Satan can't stand healthy, connected relationships inhabited by healthy people who are growing in God....* Separating and isolating people can make them easy to destroy. 📖

5. In what ways today do you see people becoming more isolated from others? Why is this isolation fertile territory for Satan's destructive agenda?

Satan is synonymous with the magnification of negative emotions. Because we are what we think and do what we think, Satan loves to play with negative emotions by magnifying them.... He is the crown prince of suggestions, and his timing is impeccable. They will come when your emotions are at a fever pitch, because it's at those moments when your desire to think is low and your desire to act on your emotions is high.

6. What negative emotions plague you most? After studying Satan's tactics, how do you think he is involved when your emotional buttons get pushed?

[Satan] is synonymous with a hurried pace of life.... Instead of living your life from a set of God-ordered values, you find that Satan encourages the activity-driven life versus the purpose-driven every time. He says success isn't living out your values, it's maintaining your image and making sure you're a part of all the urgent matters you have to get to.

7. I know that one hurts! What do you notice about the quality of your relation-ship with God when you get really busy?

📖 The Bible tells us that believers are at risk of being bamboozled by Satan's masks. He projects his character onto you by planting thoughts that sound posi-tive but produce devastating effects. Search out his file and study it so you won't lack the wisdom and intuition to see him. 📖

Discerning the Devil

1. Recall a situation where you were suckered by the Devil. What did you learn about his deceptive abilities in that circumstance?

📖 A fighting God's man must begin by being dedicated to discerning the Devil. The Bible *assumes* Satan's clear and dangerous presence in the affairs of men and reveals his person and character so that we can nail him. This is our training and our calling. 📖

2. What are some ways you can become more discerning about Satan and manifes-
tations of evil?

Here's a list of some of the qualities we encounter in others and ourselves that
should sound the warning alarm that Satan is lurking in attitudes, words, or
actions:

- murderous intent
- lies and self-deception used to justify doing the wrong thing
- self-interest and self-gratification at the expense of others
- mental diversion and distraction to eliminate spiritual transformation
- many words to mask a lack of integrity
- God's plan hijacked by man's passions and plans
- opposition to the advance of the gospel in a man's life

3. Are there other items you would add to this list—any places where you have
observed, *Satan's behind this?*

📖 When God's man sees the character of Satan and distinguishes between the
manipulator and the person being manipulated, it is a huge blow to Satan's
work.... Satan hates to be seen. Jesus knew this. That's why He never entered

situations with His radar turned off. He knew Satan would always show up one way or another.... The way Jesus met them was by first *knowing Satan's character and how it manifested,* and then by simply *calling him out.* Being familiar with Satan as a living being with a personality and character that are both recognizable and confrontable is the name of the game.

 **Fight Drill**

Remember

Submit yourselves, then, to God. Resist the devil, and he will flee from you. (James 4:7)

Reflect

1. Why is submitting to God the most important step of all in preparing to do spiritual battle?

2. How do you go about resisting the Devil? (For insight, analyze how Jesus used Scripture to resist Satan, as revealed in Matthew 4:1–11 and Luke 4:1–13.)

Respond

During the coming week, in situations where you are being tempted to give in to Satan's negative influences, practice submitting to God and resisting Satan. Keep your Bible handy in order to find scriptures that confront the Devil's lies with God's truth.

 ## Fight Reconnaissance (Man to Man)

Take turns asking each other the following questions:

1. Review the events that have happened in your lives since you last met.
2. In past and recent personal experiences, where have you seen great evidence of Satan's influence?
3. What level of success have you had in exposing Satan's trickery in your life and making him flee?
4. Pray together. Boldly draw upon the power of God that is in and among you— "For where two or three come together in my name, there am I with them" (Matthew 18:20).

Fight Small Unit Tactics (Small Group Discussion)

1. In our time, where do you see the fingerprints of Satan the most?

2. Many Christians do not seem to want to know much about Satan. Why do you think they have that attitude?

3. Satan is a master at deception. In what ways have you seen him deceiving you and others?

4. In your own life, where do you most often see Satan's influence?

5. The apostle John wrote, "If we claim to have fellowship with him yet walk in the darkness, we lie and do not live by the truth" (1 John 1:6). What might be some examples of darkness in a man's life that would prevent fellowship with God?

6. A great way to shine light on any personal darkness is to have an honest accountability relationship with another godly man. Does anyone have a story to tell of how such a relationship saved him from falling for one of Satan's tricks?

7. Before closing this session, someone read this passage written by the apostle Peter. As you consider these verses, ask yourself, *What positive things can I do to insulate myself from the influence of Satan in my life?* Then share some ideas of how to guard yourselves from Satan's influence.

His divine power has given us everything we need for life and godliness through our knowledge of him who called us by his own glory and goodness. Through these he has given us his very great and precious promises, so that through them you may participate in the divine nature and escape the corruption in the world caused by evil desires.

For this very reason, make every effort to add to your faith goodness; and to goodness, knowledge; and to knowledge, self-control; and to self-control, perseverance; and to perseverance, godliness; and to godliness, brotherly kindness; and to brotherly kindness, love. For if you possess these qualities in increasing measure, they will keep you from being ineffective and unproductive in your knowledge of our Lord Jesus Christ. (2 Peter 1:3–8)

 Fight Orders

Here's what needs to happen before the next small group meeting:

1. Complete your personal study of session 4, which includes reading chapters 8 and 9 in *Fight*.
2. Meet with your accountability partner.
3. Complete the Fight Drill section on page 55.
4. Record your observations in the Fight Journal.

Fight Journal

_____

_____

_____

_____

_____

_____

_____

_____

_____

_____

_____

_____

_____

_____

_____

_____

_____

evil agents

This week's session is based on chapter 8, "Assassins on Assignment," and chapter 9, "Devil Winds," in Fight.

Although Satan is the architect of evil, he is not the only anti-God force we have to fight against. The apostle Paul wrote of how a part of the Devil's plan for our lives is that we get to struggle against rulers, authorities, powers of this dark world, and spiritual forces in the heavenly realms (see Ephesians 6:12). That's an evil "shock and awe" force beyond imagination! But if we don't understand the evil environment we inhabit and the workings of the forces arrayed against us, we'll be toast in our spiritual battles. Let's take a closer look at what we're up against.

 Fight Intel

📖 Like the devil winds of Southern California, there's a strong spiritual pressure system in the culture against God's man…. What we must realize is that the world's systems of thinking and being are under Satan's direction. He is the dominant and controlling influence in these systems as prince of this world. We know this because as men give themselves to these isms, they are seduced farther from God and aren't able to reconcile their worldly identities with their faith. 📖

1. How have you personally encountered the "a strong spiritual pressure system in the culture against God's man"?

2. In what areas of your life do you sense the greatest tension between the world and your faith?

📖 The Bible lays out both the pressure systems and the players in detail....

"As for you, you were dead in your transgressions and sins, in which you used to live when you followed the *ways of this world* and of the *ruler of the kingdom of the air,* the spirit who is now at work in those who are disobedient. All of us also lived among them at one time, gratifying the *cravings of our sinful nature* and following its desires and thoughts. Like the rest, we were by nature objects of wrath" (Ephesians 2:1–3). 📖

3. How would you describe the ways of this world?

4. Christians are inhabited by the Holy Spirit. What spirit inhabits those who are not believers in Jesus Christ?

    📖 These world systems are packaged and sold by Satan as popular opinions and prevailing cultural norms around the globe. This is how Satan hides. It's not the Devil, it's an outlook on life, a belief, or a perspective on things that's accepted in culture by the majority. Those norms and opinions create high-pressure cultural systems that demand conformity and exclude behaviors and beliefs consistent with faith in Christ. They're also focused on keeping you centered on self and preventing you from turning to God. 📖

5. What are some of the ideas that dominate our culture today? (For example, one would be the idea of "tolerance—everyone has a right to their own truth.")

6. Which of these dominant cultural ideas are the greatest challenge to your faith?

📖 Throughout the centuries men have tried to blend the beliefs of these systems with faith in Christ. It can't be done. Jesus told us, "As it is, you do not belong to the world" (John 15:19). That's an identity statement. A short time later, John would exhort God's men to follow suit: "Do not love the world or anything in the world" (1 John 2:15). A disciple gets this, and solid God's men have been passing it along ever since that first huddle with Jesus. God's man watches out for this system of high pressure, is aware of it, does not get caught up in it, and above all does not conform to it. 📖

7. What do you think it means, *practically*, to "not love the world or anything in the world"?

8. What are some ways to be aware of Satan's high-pressure system so that you do not conform to it?

The Flesh—Evil Up Close and Personal

To make life even more challenging, our flesh combines with the works of the Enemy:

    📖 This high-pressure system of culture is continuously spinning beliefs, behaviors, and identities specific to men. It is constant and powerful. More important, it is being directed *intentionally* toward the inviting low-pressure systems of our souls. Like a magnet to steel, the flow of evil energy is inevitable and inexorable. The high-pressure devil winds of the world are designed to flow toward one destination of low pressure. 📖

1. How would you define "the flesh"?

2. Why is the flesh such a powerful ally with Satan?

    📖 Satan was kicked out of heaven, but he rules this world and its systems. It's his version of a pseudoheaven. In the world, he can receive the worship he coveted in heaven. Leader after leader lies in the ashes of his firestorms, overwhelmed by an unseen but active foe. Add to this the accelerating drought that combines with his high-pressure system to magnify his power, and we can see how God's man can unwittingly create the context for the perfect firestorm with

- a dry spirit—a life unwatered by the Word of God
- isolation—a life unwatered by authentic and honest connections to the body of Christ
- prayerlessness—a life unwatered by humility and faith and replaced with the dry tinder of self-sufficiency and pride
- negative emotions—a life unwatered by the love, peace, patience, and joy of the Holy Spirit
- secrets—a life unwatered by the freedom only honesty with God, self, and others can provide

The spiritually dry, emotionally depleted, relationally isolated, and morally vulnerable man *will be exploited.*

3. Which of the bulleted items above cause you the most difficulty in combating your fleshly desires?

4. In your walk with God up to now, what spiritual responses and disciplines have been most effective in warring against weaknesses in your flesh?

Murderous Angelic Beings (MABs)

Although demons are discussed often in the New Testament, some Christians are reluctant to acknowledge that what I call Murderous Angelic Beings (MABs) are very much alive and well on planet Earth. Here's a summary of these vicious spirits that cause so much havoc.

📖 Demons are murderous angelic beings on assignment and under orders from Satan himself. They have a file too in the Word of God. The Scripture teaches us what we need to know about these perfect soldiers of Satan. Here are the basics every God's man should know about Satan's MABs:

- They have great personal power and passion.
- They are ordered, subordered, and coordinated within a hierarchy of power, with Satan at the top of the food chain.
- They are numerous and everywhere in the world, projecting and promoting evil influences and actions.
- They exist to target both believers and nonbelievers with malice and destructive intent.
- They attach themselves to a believer's life, seeking to control whatever area is *not* under the control and leadership of the Holy Spirit. *(Think about that one for a second.)*
- They are highly intelligent agents, intimate with Satan and emotionally close to him by virtue of their shared histories, miseries, and destinies.
- They are militarily minded and exist to conquer men, cultures, nations, and the church in order to increase Satan's control.
- They are given permission by believers to influence, control, and oppress them by compromising or compartmentalizing areas of life away from Christ's control.

- They have no authority or control over a believer who is in fellowship with the Holy Spirit.
- They are the ones we should be concerned about in our quest to be God's men and fulfill His purposes on earth. 📖

1. What is your personal response to the idea of demons? Do you find it easy or hard to believe that such beings exist? Why do you have this opinion?

2. Do you agree with the comment above that demons are "given permission by believers to influence, control, and oppress them by compromising or compartmentalizing areas of life away from Christ's control"? Why do you feel this way?

📖 One other thing—you can't "sort of" believe in demons as God's man. "For our struggle is not against flesh and blood…" (see Ephesians 6:12)…. Spiritual compartmentalization in our lifestyles—whether 5 percent or 95—ensures demonic presence and influence in our lives. Demons work overtime to ensure that the unsurrendered parts of our lives take down the whole thing. They love turning dabbling in sin into full-scale disasters and death.... The Devil and his demon recruiters prostitute good men and rob them of greatness. They do this by tapping into our broken manhood, frailties, insecurities, fears, and lack of total surrender to Jesus Christ. 📖

3. What evidence have you seen in others and yourself of demonic influences when there's compartmentalization or a lack of complete surrender to Christ?

4. Why do Satan and his cohorts find opportunities where we have wounds or weaknesses?

📖 How does God's man become less vulnerable to demonic influence and control? Easy. Drive a long blade through the heart of compromise and spiritual compartmentalization. Take away demonic footholds by surrendering to the Holy Spirit's leadership in *every area* of your life, no matter the cost... Go on the offensive.... [R]emember who we're really fighting. The Bible says it's not people, it's MABs—those murderous angelic beings. 📖

Satan's Pseudoincarnation

📖 What we need to understand about all this effort on evil's part is that Satan tries to parody and imitate God's work in a perverted way. When God creates man and seeks to lead him, love him, and bless him, Satan gets in on the act, promising the same things but delivering pain. When God becomes incarnate in the person of Jesus Christ, Satan uses demons to take forcible possession of people and become pseudoincarnate himself. When Jesus Christ resurrects from the dead and the Holy Spirit comes to permanently and rightfully dwell in believers, Satan, using his MABs, seeks an ongoing and artificial presence in the lives of believers. Instead of feeling the fellowship and agreement of the Holy Spirit, we sense the unnatural and contradictory feelings of an intruder. 📖

1. Have you ever felt that there is some type of evil intruder squatting illegally in your interior life?

📖 Demons are like terrorists attempting to nest in a foreign land—they are unwelcomed but present. They can reside in those permitted spaces of a believer's life with a destructive mission. They cannot indwell as the Holy Spirit does because that is neither their mission nor their legal right. They will, however, attempt to seize areas where there exists the smallest openness to entertain a will other than God's. 📖

2. Does an awareness of how demons operate help explain otherwise unexplainable attitudes and behaviors you have observed in yourself and others? If yes, list some examples.

Demons are patient and persistent in their quest to gradually insinuate their influence on your thinking to gain control of a piece of your life. They will work against you just as your flesh and the world will. They will encourage gray areas and complaints about discomfort or loss, and then they offer easy solutions. They will exploit your conflictedness and pounce on negative emotions with a laundry list of suggestions provided by Satan himself. They will help arrange your thinking in such a way so that sin looks *really* good and totally logical.

3. Have you had an experience where in your mind a particular sin looked really good? Do you suspect that some of your thoughts were not really your own?

📖 You know it's Satan and his murderous angelic beings when the suggestions, thoughts, fears, discouragements, temptations, and core conflicts are getting magnified in your imagination. Then there will be an offering of a reality that's better than any God is offering. It's not just a solution; it's a *voluptuous* solution—one that plays into your feelings and overrides your faith. Multiple millions of these battles are being waged right this second in the lives of people all over the world. There are no cease-fires, no lulls, no moments of relaxation, and no truces. The reason is that the ever-present flaws in your character can produce conflicts that damage your relationships with God and people. It is unceasing because we are in *their backyard,* and not vice versa. Earth is in a fallen condition where fallen angelic beings have been given power to rule over and dominate nations and men. We are in that world, and those who rule it in this short time between eternities can't stand to give up a single inch of control. 📖

4. How aware are you on a daily basis that you are living in hostile territory—the backyard of Satan and demons? How might an awareness of the pervasiveness of evil influences affect how you view the world and your role in it?

📖 Control is their deadly game, and they have great experience with the male personality and its frailties and insecurities, which helps them achieve their ends. It's this intelligence, teamwork, and relentlessness in achieving the self-destruction of men that causes us to scratch our heads when we see men morph into people we don't recognize. They go from ordinary guys to obnoxious, immoral, malicious, worldly, self-serving, or worse. Believer or unbeliever, the greatest weakness a man can have is being unaware that he has given access to a demon, because it's that blindness that will do him in. 📖

 **Fight Drill**

Remember

For our struggle is not against flesh and blood, but against the rulers, against the authorities, against the powers of this dark world and against the spiritual forces of evil in the heavenly realms. (Ephesians 6:12)

Reflect

1. In the challenges you face in daily life, what evidence confirms that you are wrestling with more than flesh and blood?

2. Are you able to determine quickly when you are having an encounter with evil? How can you become even more perceptive in sniffing out rulers, authorities, powers, and spiritual forces of evil?

Respond

Make a list of situations you commonly face where you know the battle between good and evil rages hot. Ask the Holy Spirit to help you see into that real world—the unseen spiritual dimension where there's never a cease-fire on the battlefield.

 Fight Reconnaissance (Man to Man)

Take some time to review what's going on with each other. Alternate answering these questions:

1. What temptations from cultural influences (such as the media) do you find most difficult to combat?
2. The flesh is a great enemy of a Christlike life. The apostle Paul wrote that he saw "another law at work in the members of my body, waging war against the law of my mind" (Romans 7:23). Where in your life is this battle between flesh and mind most intense?
3. What are your thoughts about the activity of demons? What personal experience, if any, have you had with demonic spirits? Share requests and pray together.

Fight Small Unit Tactics (Small Group Discussion)

1. In Ephesians 2:2 we see that Satan is responsible for the "ways of this world," which are "the world's systems of thinking and being" (see page 117 in *Fight*). What ways of this world strike you as obviously under Satan's control?

2. How do we avoid getting sucked into the ways of the world?

3. There's a spiritual terrorist cell lurking in everyone—it's called *the flesh*, and it's deeply attracted to the things of the world. In today's society, what is most tempting to men's flesh?

4. Kenny Luck writes in *Fight*, "Demons are murderous angelic beings on assignment and under orders from Satan himself." How do you respond to that statement? Do you agree or disagree with the idea that demons exist today? Give reasons for your answer.

5. Do you think demonic influence is widespread in America and other modern societies? Why or why not?

6. Regardless of our individual views on demons, we all have to deal with what Paul wrote in Ephesians 6:12:

   For our struggle is not against flesh and blood, but against the rulers, against the authorities, against the powers of this dark world and against the spiritual forces of evil in the heavenly realms.

   Share any experiences, your own or those of others, that support what this scripture says about demonic/evil activity.

7. As followers of our Master, Jesus, how should we respond to any Enemy activity?

8. The best defense against our enemy is a strong offense. Based on past experience, what offensive tactics are most effective in defeating Satan and his cohorts?

Fight Orders

Here's what needs to happen before the next small group meeting:

1. Complete your personal study of session 5, which includes reading chapters 10, 11, and 12 in *Fight*.
2. Meet with your accountability partner.
3. Complete the Fight Drill section on page 73.
4. Record your observations in the Fight Journal.

Fight Journal

_____

_____

_____

_____

_____

_____

_____

the enemy's game plan

This week's session is based on chapter 10, "Not an Enigma: Part One," chapter 11, "Not an Enigma: Part Two," and chapter 12, "Hijacked," in Fight.

Men are fundamentally driven by their emotions.

Did I get your attention with that statement? I hope so, because in fact it's in our male emotional life that so many of us surrender tactical advantage to the Enemy. As men we often deny that we are emotional beings. Nothing could be further from the truth, and such an attitude only makes us more vulnerable to Satan's tricks and games. Together, let's take a look at our emotions and how to handle them positively.

 Fight Intel

Our thoughts, and the emotions they produce, drive our lives forward for good or evil. *Satan knows this.* More to the heart of the issue, our emotions powerfully influence our perceptions of reality, and those perceptions ultimately drive our behaviors. *Satan knows this too.*

📖 The Bible not only tells us that emotions fuel our lives, it tells us that Satan is plotting to exploit them for his purposes if we don't manage them the right way. 📖

1. Do you see yourself as a person who has a lot of emotions or not? Why do you say this?

2. Men are often accused of stuffing their emotions. Do you think that's true of you or not? Why?

📖 Satan knows that men are vulnerable and frustrated over their inability to control the people and events that impact their lives. More specifically, he knows that our inability to control events can precipitate a greater inability to keep control of our emotions. Sadly, without intentional security measures, we're all easy to hijack. Study the film.

A lack of emotional control makes us vulnerable. "Like a city that is broken into and without walls is a man who has no control over his spirit" (Proverbs 25:28, NASB). An ancient city without walls was pretty much indefensible. In the same way, your life is either protected or made vulnerable by a wall of self-control over your reactions to relational events in your life. The man with "no control over his spirit" gets hijacked. 📖

3. What kind of behaviors do men reveal when their emotions are out of control?

4. Do you struggle with any of these issues?

📖 *Unconfessed resentment gives Satan power in your life.* " 'In your anger do not sin': Do not let the sun go down while you are still angry, and do not give the devil a foothold" (Ephesians 4:26–27). See the picture? There's an elephant in the room, and it gets larger by the hour when it's not acknowledged, dealt with, and eliminated from human relationships. Unresolved anger in any form puts a neon Welcome sign up for evil. Like me, you might be tempted to say, "I don't have a problem with anger." Fair enough. The problem, however, is that anger is simply the baseline emotion behind the *expressions* of irritation, aggravation, agitation, annoyance, exasperation, frustration, rage, hostility, bitterness, resentment, scorn, vengefulness, contempt, envy, jealousy, [and] coveting. Any form of anger not dealt with openly, honestly, and productively is, by default, given to Satan to use as a base of operation. 📖

5. What do you think is meant by the biblical injunction "In your anger do not sin"?

6. How does the Devil get a foothold when we do not handle our anger well?

📖 *Out-of-control emotions blind you to Satan's presence.* "Humble yourselves, therefore, under God's mighty hand, that he may lift you up in due time. *Cast all your anxiety on him because he cares for you.* Be self-controlled and alert. Your enemy *the devil prowls* around like a roaring lion *looking for someone to devour*" (1 Peter 5:6–8). Peter is talking to a group of people going through an emotionally turbulent time, and he does not want them to get hijacked in the midst of their suffering. The encouragements are straightforward and effective: "Put yourself under God's authority, relieve the pressures inside by talking to God, and raise your threat level to Red."… Like anger, anxiety has a bunch of cousins, so if you're tempted to say, "I don't struggle with anxiety," think about how worry and fear manifest themselves in various behaviors: overeating, workaholism, isolation, stress, edginess, apprehension, overcontrol, overplanning, [and] avoidance. 📖

7. Have you—or has someone you know—experienced what it's like to be devoured by the Enemy?

8. Do you struggle with anxiety or any of the anxiety cousins? How do you think you might become more able to cast "all your anxiety on him," as Peter tells us?

📖 Satan aggressively waits for men to give in to their emotions because he knows they will be as unreliable and inconsistent as those emotions *and* as easy to control. When you are low, he wants you to attach to the perception created by your emotions that all is lost, all is fatal and final. God, on the other hand, says, "I am with you in the valley of the shadow of death, no need to fear, I will walk you through this." 📖

9. List experiences where you reached out to God and He walked you through a difficult time.

Act Your Way into Feelings

📖 Remembering our identity in Christ and acting on it under pressure can be difficult, especially when emotional comfort is on the line. When we want something badly, we don't want to think. Satan knows this. That's why he wants you to *feel* your way into wrong actions versus *act* the right way into new feelings. 📖

"Now that you *know* these things, you will be blessed if you *do* them" (John 13:17). In other words, based on what God says to do, I act my way into feelings versus feel my way into actions. I know what's true and right, then I do what's true and right, and the blessing comes next. My feelings about things will change *after* I do what I know God wants me to do.

1. What does having the identity of Christ mean in your life? (See Romans 6:11 and 2 Corinthians 5:17–21 for particular insights.)

Satan's Tactics

📖 Men will go to great lengths to predict the movements of the competition in business, politics, or sports.... God's men learn to discern Satan in three ways. First, we detect him by his core character traits. He leaves fingerprints.

Seeing those characteristics manifested tips us off. By familiarizing ourselves with *who he is,* we can learn to smell the rat.... The second method is by understanding the instruments of evil that he uses to manipulate and destroy men from within and without. We learn about his networks of power, his connections and associations with cultures and men. He needs as his base of operations a world system in league with your dark impulses.... The third way we recognize Satan is by observation and study. This is warfare through hard intelligence and seeing repeated patterns. 📖

1. List some situations you've encountered where Satan was obviously involved. What observations do you have about Satan's tactics in these situations?

📖 As we've seen, the spiritual world is rife with well-engineered and malicious plots designed to gain control of men, introduce a second agenda, and produce maximum devastation. As a consequence, the game that is "on" is a game of disciplined discernment of those plots. God's man is commissioned to be about the business of predicting and preempting the Terrorist's agenda much the same way a counterterrorism agent is deployed. We are appointed to know the schemes of the Devil, called to study them, trained to discern them, and prepared to come against them.... The easy part is identifying the tactics. The hard part is knowing when and where they will be used. In many instances you can't predict the situation. You simply have to be ready to respond. 📖

2. What might being a counterterrorism agent against evil look like for you?

⌕ The Bible assumes that God's man has broken Satan's code and knows his movements in advance. "For we," Paul writes, "are not unaware of his schemes" (2 Corinthians 2:11). Only fools who *want* to be defeated fail to learn what they're in for. ⌕

3. Based on past experience, what are some of Satan's favorite schemes he's used against you?

4. How successful are you now at detecting when the Devil is messing with you?

Satan's Playbook

Here are the plays Satan runs over and over. And they all take place in the *mind*:

> 📖 *Expect mental suggestion.* Every thought that encourages you to violate the express will of God is from Satan. He understands the power of suggestion, and he knows he has a friend in you—your dark side that's begging for indulgence. Satan's suggestions are always intellectually, emotionally, sensually, or physically gratifying. His suggestions always go to your need in the moment—for something new, comforting, reassuring, satisfying, or intriguing. 📖

1. Look back on some of your recent thoughts. List an example or two of a thought that on closer examination is obviously from the Evil One.

> 📖 *Expect moral temptation....* Satan never *accidentally* tempts a man. This means his timing always coalesces with what's going on *inside a man at any given moment....* Whatever is ruling your emotions at the time will be used against you when he strikes. 📖

2. What are some of Satan's favorite ways to tempt you?

📖 *Expect mental rationalization.* Any time you're coming up with good reasons to do evil things (especially religious-sounding ones), look over your shoulder. Rationalization is Satan's most productive way of encouraging self-deception. This evil-inspired logic provides safe cover for Satan to hide himself in your thinking. 📖

3. Write down several examples of how people rationalize sin.

📖 Combating satanic deception and rationalization always starts with the willingness to have a truth encounter with God, yourself, and others. When we refuse truth, we leave the door wide open to deception and destruction.... The solution? Kill your pride and love truth till it hurts.... Let the facts speak and trust God with the solution. 📖

4. In what areas of your life do you have more difficulty accepting truth and reality?

📖 *Expect accusation from within....* A lot of us have a past, some of us have regrets, and *everybody* owns hidden self-doubts, insecurities, frailties, wounds, defects, and fears. These accessories of the fallen nature act like an adhesive for the Accuser to pin accusations on our spirits and discourage us. When a man gets a healthy dose of self-pity, self-despair, or self-condemnation, Satan arrives to *magnify* those thoughts and views to feel fatal and final. He loves to exaggerate the normal and elevate it to extremes. Like this:

- "I made a mistake" becomes "I *always* blow it."
- "I need to work on that" becomes "I'll *never* change."
- "Well, that didn't go well" becomes "Well, what did I expect?"
- "I may need some support in this" becomes "I could never talk about *that*."
- "This is making me feel overwhelmed at the moment" becomes "Life is falling apart."
- "This isn't easy" becomes "How does this always happen to me?"
- "I need to figure this out" becomes "This is just like God to do this to me."…

The end game is the same: a wedge is driven into your relationships—especially with other Christians, the people who are supposed to be there for help and healing. 📖

5. Which of the internal accusations listed above—and Satan's exaggerations—have you had to deal with?

6. How do you fight off the Enemy when he is whispering lies about you into your thoughts?

📖 *Expect accusations from Christians....* If Satan can't get you to point the finger yourself, there are plenty of other unwitting fingers available to him. The evil reality of Christians accusing and abusing other Christians is a testimony to the craftiness and tactical genius of our ancient accuser. To annihilate the church, attack God's glory, and strike a blow to Jesus, he can kill three birds with one stone by sowing division within God's people.... "You, my brothers, were called to be free. But do not use your freedom to indulge the sinful nature; rather, serve one another in love. The entire law is summed up in a single command: 'Love your neighbor as yourself.' If you keep on biting and devouring each other, watch out or you will be destroyed by each other" (Galatians 5:13–15). 📖

7. Why do you think Christians succumb so easily to the temptation to criticize one another?

📖 *Expect persecution.* When the Devil fails to tempt, deceive, or discourage you through accusation, the only avenue left is the physical.... Jesus told us that for many of God's best men, it would come to this: "Blessed are those who are persecuted *because of righteousness,* for theirs is the kingdom of heaven" (Matthew 5:10). That persecution comes from Satan against a certain quality of man.... The more righteous you become, the higher the hostility factor. We are instructed to expect it because our commitment to God in this world calls for it. "Dear friends, do not be surprised at the painful trial you are suffering, as

though something strange were happening to you. But rejoice that you participate in the sufferings of Christ, so that you may be overjoyed when his glory is
revealed. If you are insulted because of the name of Christ, you are blessed, for
the Spirit of glory and of God rests on you. If you suffer, it should not be as a
murderer or thief or any other kind of criminal, or even as a meddler. However,
if you suffer as a Christian, do not be ashamed, but praise God that you bear
that name" (1 Peter 4:12–16). Open hostility in enemy territory is not unusual,
it's to be expected. 📖

8. Have you endured a painful trial on behalf of Christ? Briefly record the details
   and the outcome of the trial.

Praise God—the truth is that because of what Christ has done for us, "we are more
than conquerors" (Romans 8:37). Here are some ideas on how to defuse Satan's
schemes:

> 📖 Tell God what's going on inside and how you feel.... Then find a promise
> in the Scripture you can stand on (Romans 8:28 is great start) and surrender
> your will in the situation to God's. Follow this up by turning to a safe friend
> (spouse, if you're married) who will listen and who loves the Lord. Many times
> all you need to do is talk it out to see things aren't as bad as you felt. Receive
> the comfort of God's promise to redeem the situation and listen to what your
> friends have to say. 📖

9. Are you doing this? What results have you seen?

 **Fight Drill**

Remember

Like a city that is broken into and without walls is a man who has no control over his spirit. (Proverbs 25:28, NASB)

Reflect

1. What do you think it means to have control over your spirit?

2. How well do you control your emotions?

Respond

This week pay particular attention to how you handle your emotions. Make note of any times Satan messed with your feelings in order to make you less effective in carrying out God's will.

 ## Fight Reconnaissance (Man to Man)

1. Catch up on events since you last met. Share concerns and answers to prayer.
2. In what emotions are you most vulnerable to Satan's suggestions, accusations, tricks, and so on?
3. How can you better respond to Satan's temptations in your emotions?
4. Share individual requests and pray for each other.

 ## Fight Small Unit Tactics (Small Group Discussion)

1. Do you think men are good or not so good at dealing with emotions? Give reasons for your answer.

2. Anger, in particular, is an emotion that makes men struggle. Why do you think the inappropriate expression of anger is such a temptation to many men?

3. One of Satan's favorite ploys is to call into question the reliability of God and His Word. Which of the Enemy's lies have you encountered? Which ones were the most enticing?

4. "There's no escape from the testing ground of temptation. God said it would come—and in fact, it's necessary in order to develop a real man," Kenny Luck says in *Fight*. How have you seen temptation as a testing ground in your life? What have been the results?

5. What patterns have you seen related to your most challenging temptations? For example, are there certain situations, locations, or people that make it tough for you to resist?

6. How can you proactively defeat your toughest temptations?

7. How can God's men support one another better in order to reduce Satan's effectiveness?

 Fight Orders

Here's what needs to happen before the next small group meeting:

1. Complete your personal study of session 6, which includes reading chapters 14 and 15 in *Fight*.
2. Meet with your accountability partner.
3. Complete the Fight Drill section on page 92.
4. Record your observations in the Fight Journal.

Fight Journal

_____

_____

_____

_____

_____

_____

_____

_____

_____

_____

_____

_____

engage the enemy

This week's session is based on chapter 14, "Fix Bayonets!" and chapter 15, "Yield to Wield," in Fight.

Congratulations! You're ready to explore the deeper personal tactics in the fight with evil. When a soldier has received the proper instruction and training and is fully equipped, he's ready to fight. We've gone to spiritual boot camp, learned about the war and our enemy, gone through some training, and received our equipment.

Now it's time to engage the Enemy.

 Fight Intel

📖 In war, when a regiment is given an assignment to carry out a frontal assault across open ground or to take a hill, there is a pause *and* a quickening of the warrior. His duty is his alone. The consequences, if he is realistic, are in God's hands. All he knows is that he's getting called into close quarters with the enemy, and he needs to discharge his duty to his country, to the cause, and to his comrades. This is the reality of every warrior. He knows he is called by God to combat evil, many times in close quarters, wherever he's been assigned. 📖

1. Are you comfortable with the idea that you are God's warrior and need to enter combat with evil? Why or why not?

📖 The field of battle is inconsequential. Whether he's in a remote village in southern Mexico, with the remote in his hand defending against a screen full of porn, or looking into the remote eyes of a lost soul, he brings his *all* to the battle. He's called to fight that particular battle, or God wouldn't have placed him there. As long as he's breathing, he's fighting—right where he lives. 📖

2. What are the spiritual battles you face now, right where you live?

3. Do you feel you are properly equipped to fight these battles? List reasons for your answer.

📖 God's man knows evil is swimming below the water lines of visible reality. His daily duty is to fix bayonets in personal fields of battle right *now.* His orders stand as follows until he is called home:

"Finally, be strong in the Lord and in the strength of His might. Put on the full armor of God, so that you will be able to stand firm against the schemes of the devil. For our struggle is not against flesh and blood, but against the rulers, against the powers, against the world forces of this darkness, against the spiritual forces of wickedness in the heavenly places. Therefore, take up the full armor of God, so that you will be able to resist in the evil day, and having done every-thing, to stand firm" (Ephesians 6:10–13, NASB). 📖

4. How do you think God's man goes about being strong in the Lord?

5. What schemes do you sense the Devil likes to direct against you?

📖 The word "struggle" in my Greek New Testament is the word *palē* (PAW-leh). It means "all-out," hand-to-hand, foot-to-foot, wrestling/boxing match. In the first century, wars were not fought remotely by merely pushing buttons or from the air by firing missiles. There was only one kind of fighting—with muscles. The assumption is that God's man fights in close quarters against evil. Human effort is inadequate (*"be strong in the Lord and in the strength of His might"*), as are human means (*"put on the full armor"*), if the man in the contest hopes to survive the encounter. Flesh and blood may be the instruments of evil, but "powers," "world forces of this darkness," and "spiritual forces of wickedness" are the ones we're to attack, grapple with, and subdue by all spiritual means. This brand of fighting man is necessary if evil is to be uprooted. 📖

6. In your experience, what evil have you needed to fight in close quarters—evil in both others and yourself?

7. What promises of success do you find in the Scripture passage from Ephesians 6 (see above)?

8. Is there any reason you cannot be successful in your hand-to-hand combat with evil?

When God leads His men out and orders them to fix bayonets, there is something inherently eerie that happens when the command is obeyed. In a spiritual sense, the sound of the cold metal sliding from the scabbard, the loud metallic *click* of the knife locking deeply into the rifle lug, bonding with its warrior, sends a chill through the enemy. It is a different sensation. Lots of men chamber rounds in rifles, but men seldom fix naked, sharp steel to them unless a struggle to the death is imminent, *one on one*. The sight of a regiment advancing with fixed bayonets has a withering psychological effect on the enemy. Get the picture? You are the picture of this man ready to fight hand to hand, and it should be disturbing for our enemy to see you rising out of your bunker.

Spiritual High Ground

📖 In battle, you always want to be the one on the high ground. Whether in hand-to-hand combat or attacking as a unit, the decided advantage goes to the ones above. Yet when fighting evil, the high ground is not gained by physical action; it's a perception of your identity and *the authority behind it.* "Every *child of God* defeats this evil world, and we achieve this victory *through our faith.* And who can win this battle against the world? Only *those who believe* that Jesus is the Son of God" (1 John 5:4–5, NLT 2004).... The high ground in the fight against evil is authority." 📖

1. According to the verses from 1 John quoted above, how is victory over evil achieved?

2. Why is belief in the Sonship of Jesus so important in fighting evil?

📖 If there is one thing Satan does not want you to internalize about yourself, it is this: *your royal identity gives you powerful authority....* Let this sink in: your identity in Christ gives you victory. Say it, my brother. You are a victorious warrior *in Christ.* "No, in all these things we are more than conquerors through him who loved us" (Romans 8:37). Declare your identity. No matter what battle you are facing, no matter what obstacle you are encountering, and no matter what feeling you are battling, *stop fighting the battles Satan has already lost and enjoy the victory Christ has already won.*

3. Do you normally see yourself as a conqueror in Christ? Why or why not?

God's man has no authority unless he is under authority. Full power and authority are given only to sons who have released full control of their lives to Jesus Christ.

Under Authority

Because the spiritual high ground in our war against evil is not a physical location but a spiritual condition, it means that there are conditions God requires of us to use *His* authority effectively.... There is something about understanding authority that assures God when He approves His representatives. His willingness to advance His authority through a man depends on the man's willingness to accept His authority. "God removed Saul and replaced him with David, a man about whom God said, 'I have found David son of Jesse, a man after my own heart. He will do everything I want him to do'" (Acts 13:22, NLT 2004). The key words here are "removed" and "replaced." The transactional phrase is "everything I want him to do." Saul was removed because he obeyed God selectively, when it was convenient. Saul got into the bad habit of "mostly obeying," but David demonstrated that he understood God's overriding authority. Saul was ineffective because he hadn't surrendered. 📖

1. What are some examples of authority relationships in your own life?

2. Do you agree that the extent of God's power available through a man is linked to that man's willingness to submit to God's authority? State the reasons for your answer.

3. Do you struggle with any areas where you are tempted to *mostly* obey?

Certainly the Roman centurion is one of the best examples of submission to authority shown in Scripture. This is what the man said to Jesus:

📖 " 'I did not even consider myself worthy to come to you. But say the word, and my servant will be healed. For I myself am a man under authority, with soldiers under me. I tell this one, "Go," and he goes; and that one, "Come," and he comes. I say to my servant, "Do this," and he does it.' When Jesus heard this, he was amazed at him, and turning to the crowd following him, he said, 'I tell you, I have not found such great faith even in Israel.' Then the men who had been sent returned to the house and found the servant well" (Luke 7:7–10). It all coalesces in this scene with a man who is not yet even a follower of Christ. Go figure: a man who fights for a living *gets it*. In his world, submission to authority and the exercise of authority are inseparable. His men respond because they are under him and, at the same time, placed over others to exercise his authority. 📖

4. Why do you think the Roman centurion exhibited so much faith in Jesus?

📖 Find a great spiritual warrior, and I will show you ruthless submission to the will of God in that man's life. A rebuke of evil from a God's man who is unsurrendered or compartmentalized, or who has mixed motives, is like an attack on a navy destroyer with a squirt gun—ill-advised. God knows the condition of our submission and refuses to chamber rounds of His power and authority in a man where there's a lack of spiritual integrity. Even worse for *that* man is that evil can smell an actor.... Integrity and authority are inextricably linked.

Yielding to God's authority *in your life* green-lights the wielding of his authority *through your life*." 📖

5. Why are integrity and authority linked so tightly?

6. Think of an example of a strong Christian man you know personally. How would you describe the level of this man's submission to God's authority in his life?

Yield to Wield

📖 God's man has an infinite power to wield. But to do it, he needs to *yield*. God knows it when He sees it. So does Satan. Practically, this means dealing with the footholds in your life, those areas of behavior or character where permission or power is given to Satan to traffic in darkness…. Identifying these areas is not hard. They are the areas that harm your relationships with God and people on a consistent basis. 📖

1. Are there any areas in your life that bring harm to your relationships with God or others? List them.

📖 God's man goes after *those areas* now by yielding to a *strong step of repentance* in each area. Here's how:

- announcing your opposition to evil in prayer out loud
- asking God to show you areas of your life where you do not like or want His authority. Ask Him, Where is there tension over Your control in my life? Where am I unwilling to go? What process am I resisting? Write down on paper what comes to mind.
- accepting responsibility for that tension and admitting that sin to God and to others
- affirming God's presence and His blessings in your life and submitting yourself to His total authority
- asking Him if there's anyone you harbor bitterness or resentment toward, confessing the sin of unforgiveness, and releasing that person for what he or she has done
- disciplining your mind by ordering it according to God's Word, committing it to aggressive management, and loving God with your thought life

- declaring war against any habitual sin by inspecting it with the light of His Word. Seeing it for what it is: sin. Owning it and amputating it from your life (read Mark 9:43–47 for the protocol). And your lifestyle is permanently, visibly altered. 📖

2. Why is repentance often so difficult? Why is it always so important?

3. As you review the bulleted list above, ask the Holy Spirit to point out to you any of the items that need your attention.

📖 Footholds can be small, but when left unaddressed they can grow. All the behaviors above reflect a change of mind, an awareness of reality and truth, and a response consistent with your identity in Christ. More to the point, these are *fighting behaviors* that send a strong and clear message that you possess a new commitment to being *under* God's authority to be a better steward *of* His authority. 📖

4. In what ways do you desire to be a better representative of God's authority in the world?

Study God's men throughout history, and you'll understand why it's both necessary and practical to be engaged in the fight against evil. Look at Israel during the lives of two of its best fighters: Moses and Joshua. Look at their activity and study their spiritual health, and you will quickly see a powerful fact shine forth: as the Israelites fight and battle for kingdom advance, they have *no time or energy for sin.* Now study the times following this in the book of Judges, when they forgot their identity, laid down their swords prematurely, and blended in with the Canaanites. Israel strays from God and rebels against His lordship. Here's the point: When they *perceive* that all is well, all is not well with God's people. When God's people are free from war, they *sin.* The fight stimulates dependence, provides focus, and gobbles up ground. Less fight, more sin. More fight, less sin. It's that simple. So, God's man, fix bayonets!

5. Have you found it to be true in your experience that when God's people are free from war, they sin?

6. What can you do to stay attentive to spiritual battles in order to avoid falling to temptations to sin?

 **Fight Drill**

Remember

All authority in heaven and on earth has been given to me. Therefore go and make disciples.... And surely I am with you always, to the very end of the age. (Matthew 28:18–20)

Reflect

1. As followers of Jesus Christ, why do we never need to give in to fear or anxiety?

2. As we go about making disciples, why is it so reassuring to know that all authority has been given to Jesus?

Respond

This week identify one or more areas in your life where you have not acknowledged that Jesus has full authority.

 Fight Reconnaissance (Man to Man)

Recap with each other any significant events of the past week. Ask each other the following questions:

1. What successes have you experienced in battling evil? What concerns or questions do you still have about your role or tasks?
2. Do you feel adequately equipped to be a spiritual warrior? If not, where do you feel deficient?
3. Share any prayer requests and needs and pray for each other.

Fight Small Unit Tactics (Small Group Discussion)

1. Remember Dave Grossman's illustration about the sheep, wolves, and sheep-dogs? Do you agree with the assertion that many men in the church are sheep—"mild, placid, calm, grazing"? Why or why not?

2. God's men need to be sheepdogs—the ones who rise up to protect sheep from wolves: "God's man is dangerous and good." What does it look like in day-to-day life for a man—as a husband, father, or employee, for example—to be dangerous and good as it relates to the spiritual battle?

3. In this workbook session we studied the truth that every child of God has tremendous authority over evil because of what Christ did on the cross. Why is it, then, that so many Christians seem intimidated by Satan and evil?

4. Our authority over Satan and the forces of evil is based on one thing only—the name of Jesus. Why do you think praying in the name is so powerful? (See Mark 16:17–18 and John 14:12–14 for clues.)

5. Ask a group member to read Ephesians 6:13–18. Then discuss this question: Practically speaking, how do you actually put on the full armor of God?

6. Here's a list of the armor of God. Which of these are more comfortable for you in waging war with evil? Which are more difficult to use?
   - belt of *truth*
   - breastplate of *righteousness*
   - feet fitted for the *gospel of peace*
   - shield of *faith*
   - helmet of *salvation*
   - sword of the *Spirit*

7. Fighting men do not have time to sin. In your spiritual journey, how important is it for you to stay tightly focused on doing what God asks you to do? What happens when you don't?

 **Fight Orders**

Here's what needs to happen before the next small group meeting:

1. Complete your personal study of session 7, which includes reading chapters 16 and 17 in *Fight*.
2. Meet with your accountability partner.
3. Complete the Fight Drill section on page 110.
4. Record your observations in the Fight Journal.

Fight Journal

_____

_____

_____

_____

_____

_____

_____

_____

_____

_____

_____

_____

_____

_____

_____

_____

_____

_____

know your weapons

This week's session is based on chapter 16, "Armed and Extremely Dangerous: Part One," and chapter 17, "Armed and Extremely Dangerous: Part Two," in Fight.

If you joined the U.S. Army's Seventy-fifth Ranger Regiment, one of America's elite fighting units, your training would include using many of the following weapons: M4 and M16 carbines; an M240B machine gun; an M24 sniper rifle; an 84-mm Ranger Antitank Weapons System (RAWS); 60-, 81-, and 120-mm mortars; a Remington 870 pump shotgun; an M203A grenade launcher; and the Stinger missile.*

As a soldier of the Lord in battle against Satan and evil, you will need similar familiarity with an extensive array of spiritual weapons. So follow me to the firing range for some target practice.

---

* See Russ and Susan Bryant, *Weapons of U.S. Army Rangers* (St. Paul, MN: Zenith, 2005).

Fight Intel

📖 "We are human, but we don't wage war with human plans and methods. We *use* God's mighty weapons, not mere worldly weapons, to knock down the Devil's strongholds" (2 Corinthians 10:3–4, NLT 1996). I want them to know that a Christian is never out of the fight, because he has weapons that are lethal beyond this world. Mighty weapons of divine power to demolish evil. Isn't that every man's dream? You would think…. The Bible teaches that God's weapons were created to be used. *Used.* Versus what? Indulge me here:

- used versus *talked about*
- used versus *ignored*
- used versus *studied*
- used versus *debated*
- used versus *avoided*
- used versus *preached*
- used versus *misused*
- used versus *passed over*

I don't mean to rant about this, but far too often we men like to think of ourselves as Christ-loyal, but we don't want to use our weapons…. [W]e'll have an eternity to swap stories together, so let's start talking about how to use these babies in our fight against evil. 📖

1. In your experience, do you agree or disagree that Christian men are reluctant to aggressively use spiritual weapons against the Devil and his cohorts? Elaborate on your answer.

2. Kenny says, "We must become masters at confronting and dealing with evil." Are you fully committed to this task? Why or why not? Do you believe it's critically important or are you still unsure? Explore your answer.

One of the main goals of this discussion is to deepen our sensitivity to one profound fact: weapons are only as good as our training… [E]very effort you make to integrate and use God's weapons in your life counters evil. More important, it causes Satan and his agents to retreat, redeploy, and rethink their game plans. That's the way we like it. Instead of God's man retreating, we can have a new strategy: put evil on the run. Sounds better, doesn't it? *That's* what happens when we decide to use these weapons.

Spiritual Weaponry

God's arsenal contains a vast assortment of weaponry designed to destroy the works of the Devil. In this session, we'll look at a select group of eight weapons every man serving in God's elite special forces should know intimately and train with constantly.

Awareness of Your Position in Christ

As we've seen, knowledge of evil and of your position in Christ is the first weapon used in this fight. Not only does Satan try to keep intelligence and awareness about himself limited or misguided, he has the same objectives with your spiritual position and *the authority it commands.* Just saying "I am in Christ" is a blow to him.... It's the key that unlocks the door to spiritual power.

"I pray also that the eyes of your heart may be enlightened in order *that you may know* the hope to which he has called you, the riches of his glorious inheritance in the saints, and *his incomparably great power for us who believe....*" (Ephesians 1:18–19).

1. In your own words, describe who you are in Christ.

2. How closely does your description of your true position in Christ match how you see yourself on a daily basis at work, home, with friends, and so forth? What adjustments do you need to make?

So, God's man, when you get a chance, tell him like you mean it, and mean it as you say it: "I am in Christ. My identity has been eclipsed. I have been deputized with full authority. I personally acknowledge, accept, and appropriate that authority in Jesus' mighty name." 📖

Pray in Christ's Name

📖 When I meet men in the community and invite them to our weekly men's meeting, I tell them, "Come this Thursday morning, and I'll buy you breakfast. Just tell them, 'Pastor Kenny is treating me to breakfast this morning,' and you'll be good to go." My name is all they need to say at the chow line because it stands for *my position* and *my authority* as a pastor in my church. Requests authorized by Jesus are honored when you pray in His name. God's man speaks against the forces of darkness in a language *they understand*. When in doubt, just say the name. 📖

3. Explore why the name of Jesus the Christ is so powerful. Review these Scripture passages for insights:

In the past God spoke to our forefathers through the prophets at many times and in various ways, but in these last days he has spoken to us by his Son, whom he appointed heir of all things, and through whom he made the universe. The Son is the radiance of God's glory and the exact representation of his being, sustaining all things by his powerful word. After he had provided purification for sins, he sat down at the right hand of the Majesty in heaven. So he became as much superior to the angels as the name he has inherited is superior to theirs. (Hebrews 1:1–4)

And whatever you do, whether in word or deed, do it all in the name of the Lord Jesus, giving thanks to God the Father through him. (Colossians 3:17)

4. What situations are you facing in your life right now in which you need to ask God for assistance *in the mighty name of Jesus?*

Comply with Your Conscience Quickly

📖 Your conscience is a front-line missile defense system installed by God for your fight against evil.... [Y]our conscience can be injured by not correctly responding to it in a timely manner. Habit kills. The Holy Spirit will always validate and urge you to make good on your conscience's warnings, prompting you to go back, and not put it off. 📖

5. Can you think of a time or two when you benefited by being obedient to your conscience? How about a time when you didn't listen? What were the results?

Appropriate and Cooperate with the Holy Spirit Daily

📖 The Bible says to do only two things when it comes to the Holy Spirit: appropriate and cooperate. We appropriate His leadership, influence, and control daily by simply placing ourselves under His control. It doesn't matter whether you're a pastor or a brand-new believer. All of us must practice this daily discipline to win against evil. We "turn on" what's already inside by saying, *Holy Spirit, I surrender to Your control today. Lead me, guide me, and control me....* It's a *power* issue: "I pray that out of his glorious riches he may strengthen you with power through his Spirit in your inner being" (Ephesians 3:16). 📖

6. How would you describe the power of the Holy Spirit operating in you in your day-to-day experience?

7. In what more powerful ways would you like to see the Holy Spirit operating in you?

God's Word

📖 Roman soldiers exercised and trained heavily with the sword. More specifically, they were trained to thrust the sword versus cut with it. In fact, they made fun of those who preferred the cut to the thrust, and they relished a battle of styles.... A *thrust* accomplished the job, where cutting gave the enemy a second chance. The author of Hebrews shows that he also was intimate with a sword and how the sword of God's man is best wielded in battle: "The word of God is living and active. *Sharper than* any double-edged sword, it *penetrates* even to dividing soul and spirit, joints and marrow; it *judges* the thoughts and attitudes of the heart" (Hebrews 4:12).... [T]he end result of a strong thrust of God's Word is a *judgment. That* is what God's man is after in his fights with deception, temptation, and accusation on a personal level. And *that* is what he's after in a direct confrontation with evil.... God's man defends himself by moving into a blow with the shield of his faith, positioning the sword of God's Word, and thrusting it into the heart of evil."

8. In order to use the sword of God's Word, we need to know God's Word. How would you rate your knowledge of Scripture?

_____ Excellent

_____ Good

_____ Fair

_____ Poor

9. What can you do to improve your knowledge of the sword of God's Word? Is a new level of commitment required here?

Truth

📖 There are two forces alone that shape and influence the hearts of men: *truth* and *lies*. Whatever wins that battle for a man's heart wins the battle for his character.... That's why we see Jesus defining Himself as *truth* and *life*. Satan is Jesus' exact opposite: "the father of lies" (John 8:44) and the one "who holds the power of death" (Hebrews 2:14). And man is caught in the cross fire. The more we live in the truth, the more freedom we experience with God and people. The more we swallow the lies, the more slavery we experience in our flesh. This is why Jesus put in to His Father a special request for us before leaving Earth. Praying for His present and future disciples, He asked God to "make them holy—consecrated—with the truth" (John 17:17, MSG). 📖

10. What are some of the lies Satan tells you?

11. What truths from Scripture counter these lies of Satan?

📖 In the end, every encounter you'll have with evil is a *truth encounter*. Truth will confront the lie as good confronts evil, as the Holy Spirit confronts the flesh, and as God's Word confronts the world's values. 📖

The Blood

📖 We are in the deepest possible debt to God for the blood of His Son on our behalf.... Satan was defeated by the blood; you were cleansed by it. Satan was betrayed by it; you were rescued by it. Satan was humiliated by it; you were exalted by your trust in it. The mention of the blood is repellent to him.... For Satan, the blood is synonymous with the sacrificial death of Christ. It triggers his nightmares. Jesus snatched the victory from Satan when he believed he had Jesus' certain defeat. It's a Hall of Fame moment for Christ, a Hall of Shame moment for Satan.... So, God's man, that's your cue. Sing it. Pray it. Declare it. Remember it through deep communion. Do what you must do to remind the Great Loser of why he lost: that's right, *the blood.* 📖

12. Meditate on the following verses, which explain the primary role of the blood of Jesus in every believer's life: "For you know that it was not with perishable things such as silver or gold that you were redeemed from the empty way of life handed down to you from your forefathers, but with the precious blood of Christ, a lamb without blemish or defect" (1 Peter 1:18–19).

13. Record in the Fight Journal the specific reasons why you're thankful for the precious blood of Christ.

Prayer

📖 [T]he Bible says that Jesus has your back and is ready and willing to war with you and for you—*if you just ask.* "I urge, then, first of all, that requests, prayers, intercession and thanksgiving be made for everyone—for kings and all those in authority, that we may live peaceful and quiet lives in all godliness and holiness. This is good, and pleases God our Savior, who wants all men to be saved and to come to a knowledge of the truth. For there is one God and *one mediator between God and men, the man Christ Jesus*" (1 Timothy 2:1–5). 📖

14. What do these verses say to anyone who maintains that there are many ways to God?

📖 All prayer centered on Jesus Christ is powerful prayer. Makes sense now, doesn't it, why prayer is one the most difficult disciplines to develop as God's man? Satan pulls out all the stops, engineers interruptions, rationalizations, and other diversions—anything to keep you from getting on your knees and connecting with the God of the universe.… Your decision to pray sends shivers through the world of evil because, once again, this is a language they *understand and fear* deeply. More to the point, they know who's going to show up on your behalf. 📖

15. Do you find it challenging to pray faithfully and consistently? How might you remove any roadblocks to prayer?

16. Why do Satan and the demons fear your prayers?

Satan's Sniffles

📖 Satan has allergies. Spiritually speaking, there are behaviors that short-circuit his tactics and seriously irritate his system. More and more these days, I find that when I'm actively expressing the following character qualities in my life, the more protected I am against the Devil's tactics—and the more allergic to me he must feel. These are all strengthening disciplines for God's man and weakening influences for the Enemy.

- *Humility.* This character quality is the antigen of pride and stimulates the production of spiritual antibodies: faith, surrender, and willing submission to God's will....

- *Forgiveness.* This behavior releases you from the grip of bitterness, resentment, and anger....

- *Gratitude.* If you don't have an attitude of gratitude, then all you have is *attitude.* Apply liberal amounts of gratitude to your daily life because nothing else kills pride like gratitude....

Like me, you've probably got a lot of training to do to be a complete fighting man. I'm hit-and-miss on several of these disciplines at any given moment. The goal is to rearrange my life in such a way that using these weapons becomes a *lifestyle.*

1. Which of these qualities do you most need to increase in your life—humility, forgiveness, or gratitude? What can you do right away and over the long term to increase these qualities in your life?

 **Fight Drill**

Remember

We are human, but we don't wage war with human plans and methods. We use God's mighty weapons, not mere worldly weapons, to knock down the Devil's strongholds. (2 Corinthians 10:3–4, NLT 1996)

Reflect

1. Which of God's weapons do you need more practice with so you can be more effective in warfare?

2. What are some of the Devil's strongholds in people you know or situations you are familiar with? Are there any strongholds in your life?

Respond

Based on material in this workbook session, choose at least one of God's warfare weapons to train with and use in battle this week.

Fight Reconnaissance (Man to Man)

Debrief each other on events of the past week. Take turns sharing answers to these questions:

1. Is it easier for you to talk about spiritual warfare than to actually fight evil? Why do you think that is?
2. Which of the eight weapons against evil listed in this session seem most effective to you (awareness of position in Christ, pray in Christ's name, complying with conscience, appropriation and cooperation with the Holy Spirit, God's Word, truth, the blood of Christ, prayer)?
3. Which other weapons do you want to become more proficient in using?

Close in prayer.

 ## Fight Small Unit Tactics (Small Group Discussion)

1. What would tend to stop a man from boldly entering battles against Satan and evil?
2. Do you feel you are adequately equipped to take on the Devil and his agents? Why or why not?
3. There are many weapons God has provided to His men for effective warfare. Three of these are God's Word, prayer, and the Holy Spirit. Which of these weapons are you more comfortable using? less comfortable?
4. In His epic temptation/battle in the desert before He began His ministry, Jesus repeatedly slammed Satan with the words "it is written." Why is knowing the Word of God so critical in our fight with evil?

5. Ephesians 6:18 reads, "And pray in the Spirit on all occasions with all kinds of prayers and requests. With this in mind, be alert and always keep on praying for all the saints." How often should we pray? What kinds of requests can we bring to God?

6. Jesus said, "And I will ask the Father, and he will give you another Counselor to be with you forever—the Spirit of truth" (John 14:16–17). Why is the Holy Spirit such a key weapon in our arsenal against evil?

7 In *Fight* we read, "The battle to be a man of truth is a battle fought on many fronts. He is able to be honest with God, able to be honest with himself, and able to be honest with others." How difficult is it for you to be honest with God? with yourself? with others?

8. Why is honesty such a key character quality in God's warriors?

 ## Fight Orders

Here's what needs to happen before the next small group meeting:

1. Complete your personal study of session 8, which includes reading chapters 13 and 18 in *Fight.*
2. Meet with your accountability partner.
3. Complete the Fight Drill section on page 146.
4. Record your observations in the Fight Journal.

 ## Fight Journal

_____

_____

_____

_____

_____

_____

_____

_____

_____

_____

_____

_____

8

final orders

This week's session is based on chapter 13, "Evil Loves Religion," and chapter 18, "The Ultimate Weapon," in Fight.

You're nearing the completion of your training. You've acquired skills and a deeper understanding of the Enemy's tactics for the fight. In this final session together, I want to point out a deadly pitfall for many devoted soldiers of Christ—*religion.* That's right, our enemy—the Master Deceiver—loves it when a God's man substitutes the rules and regs of religion for the dynamic, moment-by-moment promptings and direction of the Holy Spirit. Of course "religion" in itself is not bad. But there's little more disruptive to the forces of good in this world than a group of religious people who set up requirements for people to get to Jesus. Remember Jesus' choice words for these devotees who took the wrong road:

> Woe to you, teachers of the law and Pharisees, you hypocrites! You give a tenth of your spices—mint, dill and cummin. But *you have neglected the more important matters* of the law—*justice, mercy and faithfulness.* You should have practiced the latter, without neglecting the former. You blind guides! You strain out a gnat but swallow a camel. (Matthew 23:23–24)

Trust me—you don't ever want to be caught munching on a camel burger! I hope you're with me.

 Fight Intel

📖 Amazingly, in our fight, it's possible for even the inertia created by our salvation to be manipulated and thrown off course. Though we might fully embrace the gospel and God's power in our lives, slight trajectory and velocity changes of the mind, over enough time, can pull our vessels way off course. I know. It doesn't seem fair. And it isn't. But just like the imperiled space capsule had to fire its engines at exactly the right times to keep the right trajectory, God's man must employ constant vigilance to listen to the right voices and use the indicators to steer toward an authentic, Christ-centered life. Satan makes well-calculated attempts to take advantage of our spiritual passion and momentum to slingshot us away from God's highest purposes and toward his own target of a *synthetic* "Christian" life. That target, as the name suggests, has the look of faith but none of its power. 📖

1. Why is your mind always of utmost importance in staying sharp as a warrior for Christ?

2. Have you experienced being pulled slightly off target in your Christian walk?

If so, describe what happened and how you got back on course.

📖 Think about it. Have you seen this before? A Christian with good intentions in fact ends up spreading corruption through his self-serving "acts of service," never suspecting he's the least bit off track. It is possible for evil to masquerade as good under the cover of religion without the person even realizing he's doing wrong. Sure, he might wonder where his blessings are or sense there's something missing in his joy. But take a look at the next Fight Fact: Satan knows that good intentions, just a little off, can cause significant damage. 📖

3. Recall a situation when you were certain you were saying or doing the "right thing," but the results were not positive. How did your intentions being "just a little off" create a problem?

📖 When I converted to Christianity, there was never a discussion among Satan and his agents lamenting or complaining that they had "lost another one" to Jesus. On the contrary, *real evil* is much more vigilant and intelligent. Satan can take the soft dough of our faith and twist it into a thing of harm. He is undaunted in his quest mainly because he has had such wild success sending people into a religious orbit.... The other, highly volatile side of me contained the accelerant material I hoped my newfound faith would magically erase. These were the unstable elements lurking in my character: patterns of thinking, mixed motives, emotional injuries in need of healing, deep insecurities, fears, longings, disappointments, shame, discontentment, and a deep-rooted need for approval and acceptance. God wanted to work those out His way over time, but what I didn't know was that Satan wanted a shot at them too. And with *me, a signed-and-sealed Christian!* How could he possibly touch me? Jesus' words to His disciples tell the whole story: "Make sure that the light you think you have is not really darkness" (Luke 11:35, NLT 1996).

4. What issues in your character have provided opportunities for Satan to pull you off track as you sought to become more like Christ?

5. Knowing yourself as only you do, what do you think might be Satan's perfect plan to bring you down?

The Dysfunctional Christian

📖 Satan's goal is dysfunctional spirituality. He's working overtime to create inauthentic, judgmental, insecure, and insulated Christians so in love with *acting* "Christian" that they don't have a clue what it means to *be* one. They're uncomfortable around people who aren't Christians, they don't know how to engage them, and they make "spiritual" excuses for not connecting with them: they're bad influences, unrepentant, making bad choices. Should people who don't know Christ already know how to act like Him? Religious attitudes confuse people and kill our compassion. 📖

1. What's been your experience—are you acquainted with Christians who struggle with *being* authentic followers of Jesus?

2. Do you see any of these negative religious attitudes in yourself?

3. We all are in process, but what are some actions you may need to take to reduce any dysfunctional tendencies in your Christian life?

📖 Religion distances people from a real relationship with a living and loving God and leaves survivors with a spiritual limp. In short, religion messes everything up. In this incredibly high-stakes war, God's man must opt out of religion and jump into the real battle for the heart and soul. 📖

4. Describe in your own words what the phrase "evil is in love with religion" means.

📖 Man-made religion is war against man and God by satanic diversion. It takes the focus off the real Enemy and puts it on man, letting bad character corrupt a good thing. It's as useful a tool as murder, lust, adultery, and idolatry. Religion is synonymous with impotence, and Satan uses it to insulate believers against true spiritual advances. 📖

5. Have you ever experienced religious activities becoming a diversion from authentic Christian living? If so, describe what happened.

📖 So how religious have you become? Are you distant from the real needs of those around you? If you're judgmental toward outsiders, afraid to get dirty, or "playing Christian" to feel better, rest assured that Satan is playing you. The way you fight this, Jesus says, is by simply being the good neighbor who walks humbly, acts compassionately, and loves mercy. If you are thinking these qualities are not manly, you're right. They're godly. 📖

6. Do you fight the tendency to distance yourself from the real needs of other people?

7. How might you become more aware of the needs of others in your life?

The Ultimate Weapon

In warfare, technology triumphs. Against evil, *our* overwhelming force is obedience.

Listen to Jesus tell His soon-to-be killers about His mission and His ultimate weapon: "I know my sheep and my sheep know me—just as the Father knows me and I know the Father—and I lay down my life for the sheep. I have other sheep that are not of this sheep pen. *I must bring them also.* They too will listen to my voice, and there shall be one flock and one shepherd. The reason my Father loves me is that I lay down my life—only to take it up again. No one takes it from me, but I lay it down of my own accord. I have authority to lay it down and authority to take it up again. This command I received from my Father" (John 10:14–18).

In obedience, Jesus modeled how God's man *always risks obedience toward his greatest hope.*

1. Why is obedience to God such a potent weapon in the spiritual fight?

Hope-filled obedience is a weapon for which the Devil has no answer and no solution. He was disarmed by it. He was disposed of by it. He was ultimately judged and his fate determined by it. He could not possess it or counter it, mitigate it, or defend against it. He couldn't detect it, deflect it, or destroy it. It was straightforward and striking, plain and powerful. Jesus Christ defeated evil, in the end, without a word of rebuke—just obedience.... Satan was overwhelmed, overcome, and overpowered by three words uttered, not on the cross, but in the Garden of Gethsemane: "As *you* will" (Matthew 26:39). The result of Christ's choice to follow God's lead was a thermonuclear disaster for the Devil. "Just as through the *disobedience of the one man the many were made sinners,* so also through the *obedience of the one man* the many will be made righteous" (Romans 5:19)....

The power of obedience over evil is overwhelming to evil when you are willing to sacrifice for your greatest hope in Christ. Jesus' deep desire was simply to bring people into relationship with God. That strong hope created an even stronger willingness to obey and fight: "I lay down my life... I lay it down of my own accord." The result: the hope of God's man fuels his *obedience* in the fight. The God-Man modeled how a strong eternal hope manifests in consistently strong choices. A weak hope manifests in weak choices. Obedience overwhelms evil, but the hope that drives obedience leads to victory. 📖

2. What is the strong hope in your life?

📖 Jesus remembered what He was fighting for, and it wasn't simply to take Satan out to the shed for a good spanking. It was because of *you.* Your future with God was the strong hope that fueled a stronger, evil-killing obedience. And because of this, evil simply could not compete with the hopeful obedience of the God-Man. Think about that, God's man: a future inhabited by *you* fueled Jesus' overwhelming obedience and defeated all attempts by evil to get Him to compromise in His quest. 📖

3. Have you recently expressed your gratitude to Jesus for His uncompromising obedience? How do you feel about the fact that He provided the way for you to be reunited with God and enjoy a never-ending life with Him?

"See to It" Victories

[My] biggest wins against evil have not been in the mission field but in the killing fields of my character—the places in me that sabotage Christlikeness and undermine my relationships with people, beginning most crucially with my wife. I call these the "see to it" areas: "See to it, then, that the light within you is not darkness" (Luke 11:35). These words of Jesus are burned on my brain mainly because they strongly indicate that God's man can *fake it*. Evil has a field day with men who do.

Just to lead out and demonstrate the importance of this, I'll share some of the "see to it" strongholds in my own life:

- surrendering my finances
- disciplining and saying no to myself for higher purposes
- confessing and confronting sexual temptation in open and accountable ways with my wife and other men
- addressing blind spots of pride
- having no secrets
- handling conflict and anger

- accepting that my identity as a man had suffered damage in my family of origin and was ripping at my marriage
- agreeing to see a counselor to defeat emotions that kept me bound to my past
- saying no to commitments to say yes to walking closer with God and strengthening relationships with people

These are just a few, but they should convince you my motives have been mixed up and the Enemy was given access. This is *my* stuff. 📖

1. What areas in your life have been "see to it" strongholds that required specific attention?

2. Are there other "see to it" areas in your character or behavior needing your attention now?

📖 While these are some of the biggies, there are also my daily skirmishes with evil that call for obedience:

- scanning the sports page rather than spending time in the Bible
- being grateful for my circumstances versus giving in to grumbling

- pausing before responding to a criticism
- expressing the discipline to say no to too many "opportunities"
- choosing forgiveness over resentment
- opening conversations with people about Jesus when prompted by the Spirit
- depending on God throughout my day instead of being self-sufficient
- not playing to people to please them or be accepted
- taking *full* responsibility when I blow it versus trying to defend myself 📖

3. Do you identify with any items on the above bulleted list? Are there issues not listed that cause daily obedience skirmishes for you?

4. List one or two daily issues where you want to be obedient. For each issue, what might you do to increase obedience?

"As You Will"

We've reached the end of our study. You're now equipped, trained with the ultimate weapon, and ready for the fight. As you go out, remember to reflect upon your personal need to surrender in every aspect of your life:

📖 Your first and most effective weapon is personal obedience to God through the character of Christ. With it, you are never out of any fight against evil. But without it, all the fundamental skills we have discussed here are absolutely *powerless.* To that end, we *must* make Christlikeness our supreme goal. From there, we appropriate more of His obedient character for more spiritual victories over evil and add more tactical weapons to our arsenal. We understand that God is more concerned that His Son's character comes forth in us than in the defeat of evil through us, because He deeply cares for our well-being. And in fact, our godly character ensures evil's defeat. 📖

1. If God is more concerned with the coming forth of His Son in us rather than the defeat of evil, what does that mean about your role in the fight with evil?

📖 It is so simple, so stunning, so beautiful, and so devastating to evil. This is our confidence for every fight we ultimately face. And there will always be another fight. The Bible says to count on it: "In fact, everyone who wants to live a godly life in Christ Jesus will be persecuted" (2 Timothy 3:12). God's plan for you is not immunity from the struggle but victory *in* the struggle. 📖

2. Have you suffered persecution for Christ and the gospel? Explain your answer.

3. How does persecution strengthen a believer?

📖 The eternal hope and drive of God's man pulls from him uncommon commitment that allows him to pray the same powerful words as his Leader: "As *you* will." Saying "as *You* will" to God says the converse to Satan, the world, and the flesh: "*Not* as you will." Pray it right now, and send the Devil packing. Pray as Jesus prayed, that you may fight as He fought and live as He lived. Launch this prayer of obedience again and again, and see how it prevails against overwhelming odds. You *will* prevail precisely because you possess the ultimate weapon. And you will take confidence in all your future battles, advancing against evil in incredible ways.... [T]he true work of fighting evil is the work only a true God's man can do. "I felt I had to write and urge you to *contend for the faith* that was once for all *entrusted to the saints*" (Jude 3). Only a saint is fit to pick a fight with evil. And you are a saint already, a title that's neither earned nor deserved. It's a matter of ownership. Believe in Christ's ownership over you, and you will be victorious. The battle has fallen to us, my friend. Go charge that hill. Heaven beckons. 📖

 **Fight Drill**

Remember

If anyone loves me, he will obey my teaching. My Father will love him, and we will come to him and make our home with him. (John 14:23)

Reflect

1. Why do you think Jesus stated that obedience was a sign of love for Him?

2. What are we promised when we choose to obey Christ's teaching? Practically, what do you think this means?

Respond

Every one of us is in the process of learning how to become more obedient. As you conclude your training, list several areas in your life where you want to increase your obedience to what Jesus taught.

Fight Reconnaissance (Man to Man)

Share what's happened in the past week. In particular, what skirmishes have you had with Satan and evil? Ask each other the following:

1. In what areas of your life do you find it difficult to obey God?
2. What are some of the more meaningful and memorable things you have learned from this study?
3. Share prayer with one another.

Since this is your last "official" time together related to this study, discuss whether you want to keep meeting regularly as accountability partners. It's a good idea to do so. Go for it!

 ## Fight Small Unit Tactics (Small Group Discussion)

1. In this session, one topic we looked at is authentic Christianity. What would you say are the qualities of an authentic Christian?
2. "God's man must employ constant vigilance to listen to the right voices and use the indicators to steer his life toward an authentic, Christ-centered life." What do you think is meant by "right voices" and "[right] indicators"?
3. First Samuel 16:7 says, "Man looks at the outward appearance, but the LORD looks at the heart." What does God look for in our hearts?
4. Some of our greatest victories against evil come in battles fought in our own character. What areas in a man's life seem to be the major sites where the battle turns toward good or toward evil?
5. Why is there such a tight relationship between success in our internal battles and success in our external battles?

6. The apostle Paul wrote to his protégé, Timothy, that "everyone who wants to live a godly life in Christ Jesus will be persecuted" (2 Timothy 3:12). How have you experienced persecution?

7. What further persecution might we experience as we become more active in opposing Satan and evil?

8. Since this is our last discussion of the *Fight Workbook,* take turns sharing what you consider to be the most memorable things you have learned in this study.

Conclude in prayer. Ask the Holy Spirit to protect your knowledge acquired through this workbook of the real spiritual struggle, to keep it from being snatched away by the Evil One.

 Fight Orders

Take time to record some final thoughts and conclusions in the Fight Journal. The Lord be with you as you fight for Him!

Fight Journal

_____

_____

_____

_____

_____

_____

_____

_____

_____

_____

_____

_____

_____

_____

_____